THE
BERLIN SHADOW

THE
BERLIN SHADOW

Living with the Ghosts of the
Kindertransport

JONATHAN LICHTENSTEIN

SCRIBNER
LONDON NEW YORK SYDNEY TORONTO NEW DELHI

First published in Great Britain by Scribner, an imprint of
Simon & Schuster UK Ltd, 2020

1 3 5 7 9 10 8 6 4 2

Simon & Schuster UK Ltd
1st Floor
222 Gray's Inn Road
London WC1X 8HB

www.simonandschuster.co.uk
www.simonandschuster.com.au
www.simonandschuster.co.in

Simon & Schuster Australia, Sydney
Simon & Schuster India, New Delhi

Image on p.3 United States Holocaust Memorial Museum,
courtesy of National Archives and Records Administration, College Park.

The author and publishers have made all reasonable efforts to contact copyright-
holders for permission, and apologise for any omissions or errors
in the form of credits given. Corrections may be made to future printings.

A CIP catalogue record for this book is available from the British Library

Hardback ISBN: 978-1-4711-6727-0
Trade Paperback ISBN: 978-1-4711-6728-7
eBook ISBN: 978-1-4711-6729-4

Typeset in Bembo by M Rules

Printed in the UK by CPI Group (UK) Ltd, Croydon, CR0 4YY

For Joe and Freddie and Rosa

The *Kindertransport* (Children's Transport) was
the informal name given to the rescue effort that
brought unaccompanied refugee children to Great
Britain between 1938 and 1940. Approximately
10,000 children made the journey from Germany,
Poland, Austria, Holland and Czechoslovakia. Most
were Jewish. One of the children who made the
journey on his own, aged twelve, was my father,
Hans Lichtenstein.

1.1

I ring. He answers.

> You want to go?
> *Yes.*

He falls silent. There's a long gap.

> The trip might help you sleep.
> *I doubt it.*
> How is it?
> *What?*
> Your sleep?

He falls silent again.

> It must be alarming.
> *What?*
> Not being able to sleep.
> *I've never been able to sleep.*
> Perhaps the journey will help your nightmares.
> *Perhaps it will make my nightmares worse.*
> But you want to go?

Yes.

And so I organise it – the trip: the dates, the ferry, the tickets, the car, the route, the passports, the hotel. Later I ring again.

We're going to do your original journey in reverse.
In reverse?
We're going to go backwards.
Backwards?
We're going to go to Berlin from here. Then we'll come back.
But I didn't go back.
I know that.
Mine was a one-way ticket.

He laughs.

I want to try to find where my father's shop was.
Of course.
And my father's grave.
Yes.
And the station?
The station too.

There. It has been agreed. I will walk the pavements with him. Together we will breathe the air of the city that ripples its past through his daily life and the corners of his children's lives, the rivulets of its history draining into us, the gutters carrying the rain and wash of its streets, its twisted papers, its yellowed stars, its broken glass, its ash, his father's grave. The station. The shop.

1.2

For many years I had wanted to travel with my father to Berlin in order to trace the route of his escape on one of the *Kindertransports*. However, the fragility of our awkward and distant relationship had made the arrangement of such a journey impossible. The thought of spending days and nights together in close proximity appealed to neither of us for we both understood that such a trip could break the small amount of fondness that had only recently arisen between us. As well as this we both knew that during such a journey my father would be forced to confront a series of darknesses he had kept, for his whole life, close to his chest. And we knew too that the illumination of these darknesses might well precipitate in him an overwhelming despair – 'a despair', he had confided to me on more than one occasion, 'I might never recover from'.

Nonetheless, as an old man, and after a debilitating illness that had begun to temper his fitful spirits, he agreed to make the journey in order to confront the event that had dominated his life. Though I had only recently begun to realise it, the event had come to dominate my life too – through my endless and repetitive cycles of a brooding need to be away from all people; an occasional, vivid and saturating experience of elation; a propensity for a violent and unsettling anger; and extreme productivity followed by months of a grey, undifferentiated torpor as well as a bleakness so frightening at times I did not want to remain alive.

Initially we chose the date of the return journey in order to mark the anniversary of my father's departure from Berlin, which he maintains was six weeks before Britain declared war upon Germany and was 'one of the last *Kindertransports* out of Berlin'. However, due to an illness that befell him that summer we settled instead on the anniversary of Kristallnacht. This was because a photograph had been found that showed his father's shop pictured after it had been smashed and looted during this catastrophic event. My father wanted to try to find the site of this shop, 'to see what's there, if anything'. He also wanted to visit his father's grave located in the Jewish Weißensee cemetery. He had never visited his father's grave, not even as a child. He had been kept away from his father's funeral and did not know that his father's death was by suicide until many years after the war had ended.

My father could not bring himself to tell me that his father had committed suicide until my eighteenth birthday. That day he made the announcement to me while we were driving together through the Welsh hills towards Cefnllys. The news arrived from out of the blue.

Now you're eighteen I have something to tell you.
What?
My father committed suicide.
Did he?

I don't want to talk about it.

How?

Shut up.

But—

I said shut up.

And so we carried on driving, him at the wheel, revving the engine, tyres whining, his attention on the bends of the road, the car leaning at precarious angles as he took the corners at speed, trimming each apex, bumping over cat's eyes, all four tyres about to lose their grip, the Welsh hills surrounding us.

1.3

Cae Hyfrydd was a dark house and full of ice in winter so that in the mornings the thin glass of the windows was crazed with frost on the inside and occasionally strange noises passed through it during the night. It had high stairs, which curved, and an attic. It was our new semi-detached house on Pentrosfa, the unmade road that rose steeply from Wellington Avenue. Pentrosfa was a road that was different to any I had experienced before; bumpy and cratered and wide. It exuded space and looking out from the window of our front room the other side of the road seemed far away. When the Evanses' son wheeled out his metallic green BSA motorbike from his parents' garage on the opposite side of the road and, hurling his weight onto the silver lever at its side, kick-started it into life, it was as though he had emerged from an exotic land, a world of detached bungalows with lawns and trimmed hedges, of white gates, of front doors with stained glass; an architecture of permanence and reliability.

Pentrosfa was an unmade road, a bastard road of cantankerous humps and angry stones. It was as though it had been built as an act of malice, impeding progress rather than advancing it. My father's solution to its array of broken surfaces was simple. Every morning he placed ashes and clinker, the waste from our coal-burning range, into its melancholy crevices. It was a ritual. First he would sweep up the cockroaches that ran around our black slate kitchen floor onto a steel shovel. Then he would open the top door of our coal-fired range and throw them into its dark-red interior. Before he threw them the cockroaches would desperately but noiselessly try to scrabble up the shovel's cold steel shaft, their mute, keratin legs flailing, entangled with each other, crossed and interwoven and jerking and frantic as they slipped back down the shovel's shaft and then further, over its scoop, as they attempted to escape the glowing flames behind them. But their struggles were futile. Although one or two dropped off the shovel and raced away, most entered hell in reverse.

Having burnt them my father would throw some more coal from the coal scuttle into the fire, close its door and then remove the stove's tinder box. This was full of the ashes of cockroaches and the burnt coal that had kept the stove alight overnight. He would carry these ashes into the road dressed only in a towel wrapped like a sarong around his waist. This brief outfit was mandatory, regardless of the weather, and neither sun nor rain, nor even thick snow, deterred him. Often as he began to fill the hole a gust of wind would whip up so that a cloud of fine ash with its swirling flecks of pearl would momentarily envelop him as he placed the ashes into the crevices, bent and concentrated, and smoothed them with his hands. Then, for a split second, he resembled a crouching apparition, the ashes of cockroaches and coal enveloping him and brushing his skin and entering his lungs and twisting past the fine dark hairs that grew in patterns on his chest.

During times of snow he was brazen, his towel flapping around his waist, his feet shoeless. From our back door his trail of footprints led out through the unmarked white, each print with its elongated second toe outlined, so that for a while his footprints inscribed the land, clearly delineated, their route marking the topography, present alongside the crisscross prints that revealed the journeys of blackbirds and thrushes and sparrows, all outlined perfectly until the gently cascading snow covered them.

The road took many years to fill and my father's journey naturally extended as he smoothed it. He had started at our back door and after a couple of years had successfully evened out the small road behind our house. Then he had to move further afield and so progressed into the centre of Pentrosfa where, particle by particle, he rebuilt it, filling holes, levelling bumps and crevices, easing journeys. The reparation of ashes. He was good to the road and the road, by accepting his ministrations, in turn was good to him.

1.4

I collect him from his house in Llandrindod with its rivers Ithon and nearby Wye, its surrounding hills and rocks, its hamlets Llandegley, Llanyre, Pen-y-Bont and Disserth, where the river pools darkly opposite the church of St Cewydd's.

He's packed and waiting. He's sitting on his large crimson suitcase in the kitchen wearing an ironed pale-grey checked shirt and olive-green moleskin trousers with ironed creases. My mother, Beryl, greets me and reads out a list of his pills, showing me various packets as she does so.

'These are for his eyes.'

Okay.

'These are for his bowels.'

Right.

'These are for his blood pressure.'

Okay.

'The pills for his eyes are important. If he doesn't take them his retinas could detach.'

Really?

'So don't forget.'

I won't.

'I don't want his retinas to detach.'
It's not something I want either.
'You wont forget, will you? It's just . . .'
What?
'I know what you're like.'

My father drums the circular kitchen table with his fingers.
My sister Jane's there. She leans towards me. She says:

'I tried to do his medical insurance but they wouldn't
do it.'
He's not insured?
'His belongings are insured.'
You've insured his belongings?
'He's so old it was going to cost a fortune; they didn't
want to do it.'
But what if something goes wrong? What if it's all too
much for him?
'It'll be fine.'
Fine? What if I lose the pills?
'You'll manage.'
What if he dies?
'You'll just have to drive him home.'
I won't be able to get through customs if he dies.
'I'm sure you'll think of something.'

Jane and my father leave the table to walk around the garden.
My mother is holding one of her teacups with flowers glazed

on it. She lifts it from its saucer then tilts her head at a slight
angle and says:

'Sometimes your father looks . . .'
What?
'Dead.'
Dead?
'Dead.'
Does he?
'Sometimes when he falls asleep he turns slightly blue
and then he can appear dead.'
Do you think he's all right?
'Not really.'
Do you think he should be doing this trip?
'Not really.'
Why didn't you say anything?
'He wants to go.'
You're sure?
'He wants to see if he can find the shop as well as his
father's grave.'

My father and I leave through the dove-grey front door and
walk to the car. He has no medical insurance. At times he
might look dead. He drags his enormous, fully insured suitcase behind him.

'I can manage my own case, thank you very much,' he
replies to my offer of help, his voice rising above the loud noise
of the suitcase's wheels as they scratch the ground.

His suitcase must have been one of those purchases where its colour in the shop looks pleasing and cheerful, but dragging it along the road and then loading it into the back of the car it looks absurdly bright and out of scale. This is the beginning of his return journey. The suitcase he should be carrying is small and brown. It should have a piece of string tied to its handle. It should have a white label attached to it. It should have a number on it written in black ink.

I walk over to a nearby hedge, pick up five stones, three small and two slightly larger, and place them in my pocket.

> *On the way back I'll take the train home from London on my own, thank you very much.*
> Of course.
> *And I want to take the train from Harwich to Liverpool Street, too.*
> No problem.
> *Preferably on my own.*

We get into my brother Simon's old car. Generously I have been given it. It is a 12-year-old bottle-green Audi estate and is, as is usually the case with my brother's possessions, towards the top of the range. It has large comfortable seats and air conditioning. Simon has had the engine 'chipped' to increase its power. He has had special suspension installed so that it can go round corners faster, and 'track in a straight line'. It is by far the nicest car I've ever had, this car of Simon's, and is ideal for the drive to Berlin.

I open Google Maps on my phone. I trace the impending journey, my fingers flicking the map across the screen. First the road to Harwich where we will catch the ferry, then across the North Sea to the Hook of Holland, then the road north towards Amsterdam, then a straight line into Germany and finally due east to Berlin. I show my father the route.

Your journey in reverse.
Yes. Yes it is. My journey in reverse.

I hear his breath catch in his throat. The sound of his inner dogs. They've woken. They've scented their prey's fragility. And they've waited long enough for this journey, clicking at his heels with their wingbacks, their tails and their dark coats.

There was a flower bell.
Sorry?
A flower bell.
A what?
A bell in the shape of a flower.
Where?
At the station.

1.5

During my early childhood my father never talked directly about his own experience of being a child, nor anything at all about his German roots. It seemed almost as though he had never been a child. He never talked about his father or his mother or his grandfathers and grandmothers. He never mentioned friends or where he played or where he lived or where he went to school, nor offered any details of any kind about his formative years. It was left to my mother to tell me one day in the kitchen of our house when I was eight years old that my father had, a few weeks after his twelfth birthday, left Berlin on his own, carrying a small suitcase. More than this she did not know herself – my father had never explained the details in full to her either. As she said, while I stood on the cold, grey, slate floor in my socks, 'He doesn't like to talk about it.'

Glimmers of information about his past would emerge when an occasional relative of his who had also escaped from Germany came to stay with us in Wales, but such visits were few and fleeting, and questions I asked were always met with the phrase, 'Mind your own business.' Now and then, information would leak out unexpectedly at home: on one occasion he remembered the texture of his mother's poppy-seed cake just as my mother served a sponge; on another he remarked on his mother's ability to keep all her plates warm while she served dinner, as my mother struggled to serve out the food she had cooked onto cold ones. Once a large box of broken cutlery arrived at our house. It had the letter 'L' inscribed upon its handles, a remnant of some family silver. It stayed in the garage, clearly agitating my father, though, as a child, I did not know why. There were other behaviours that I did not understand either – a hatred of Volkswagens and a loathing of Mercedes, so much so that if he saw either, which was an unusual event as there were hardly any on the roads in Wales at that time, he would exclaim, 'Ghastly car!', almost spitting out the words. He refused to let any of his children learn German at school, allowed no books about the Second World War into the house, made no reference to Hitler, never referred to the Holocaust and urged us on many occasions to 'steer clear of crowds'.

My father's mother, my grandmother, Ruth, survived the war. As my mother's parents had both died by the time I was two years old Ruth was my only living grandparent, but as she lived in East Berlin and was not allowed 'through the wall', and as my father could not bear her and would only talk to her once a year on the phone during the winter, I only ever met her three times, once when I was thirteen when my father took me to visit her in East Berlin and then twice more in my twenties in Wales when she was allowed out of East Germany to visit my father. There I spent a couple of hours with her, though never alone. She remained quiet as she couldn't speak

English and I couldn't speak German. At that time the questions I needed to ask her had not yet formulated themselves, meaning that I would not have been able to ask her any useful questions even if we had shared a language.

The consequence of my grandmother's absence and my father's silence about these matters was that, as a family, we unwittingly inhabited for lengths of time an unknown, inexplicable world full of silences and unspoken loss.

1.6

At its front Cae Hyfrydd had a path, which was crumbling, and so Mr Bubyage was asked to lay a new one from the garden gate to the front door. A small round Polish widower, he always brought a jar of honey to us sometime before Christmas and, if it was I who stretched up my fingers to unlatch the black-and-cream front door, it was into my hand that his jar of honey was silently delivered, its ancient colour bright in the winter light. And as he placed the jar in my hands he uttered words I did not understand, ones that were full of breath and a strange insistence. And when I then took the jar of honey and gave it to my father, he would look down on it and say, 'I wish he wouldn't bloody well do this', before placing it in a cupboard.

Mr Bubyage built the path beautifully. First he placed long planks of wood from the front door to the gate and carefully secured them by pushing wooden pegs into the soil, so marking out the outline of the path's shape. This was, he told me, 'the shuttering', and was, 'the shape the concrete will become. Concrete is the shape of the inside of the shuttering.' Much later, when the path was finished and after the concrete had set, he pulled away this wooden shuttering and showed me the marks the wood grain had left behind, now engraved on the concrete: 'The back to front of the wood's pattern.' Although his craftsmanship was faultless, the finished result was as plain as a small, straight concrete garden path can be, constructed carefully but bound by the limits of its sullen surface. In the cold mornings he would be there, casting his trowel evenly across the grey damp cement, setting a crisscross pattern, effecting a small camber so that puddles would not collect when it rained. He worked diligently and with concentration, never asking for a cup of tea and occasionally speaking to me quickly in words that I could not understand, his mode of communication the laying of concrete.

Mr Bubyage brought the building materials for the path, a morsel at a time, on a black, upright bicycle. A small wicker basket strapped onto the curved, rusting handlebars of his bike held the dry cement and a faded red saddlebag at the back contained his tools. This arrangement meant that he was continually covered in the cement dust as it eddied out of the wicker basket when he cycled, coating him in a fine pale grey from his trilby hat to his black polished shoes, the peculiar dryness of the cement dust drawing out, by capillary action, the surface moisture of his skin. He looked like a relic, something that had blown in from another world, something estranged, a library of grief upon his shoulders, the dullness of his grey skin exaggerating the effect of his bright, lonely eyes. It took him weeks to make the path, his transport being almost unbearably inefficient, but when it was done it was done and, much to my parents' puzzlement, despite his labours he refused payment.

1.7

We leave the house and drive down Cefnllys Lane slowly. We move along the quiet roads of Wales, their hedges high, their near hills a balm. We turn left in Llanelwedd, following the old railway line beside the Wye, skirt round Brecon, climb through the Beacons, see Pen y Fan where the SAS train, drive to Abergavenny and then along the Severn's tree-lined valley. We pass the ruins of Tintern Abbey, cross the Old Severn Bridge and drive along the M4. We stop at Reading Services. There we are in a different world. LCD screens, crowds, refrigerated food. We drive to the M25 then around it to the A12, then north-east until we approach the flat land near Harwich on the coast. My father sits quietly in the front seat, his gaze forward, his neck craned.

> This is the landscape you will have first seen after you
> got off the ship.
> *I suppose so.*
> The one you saw out of your train window on the way
> to London Liverpool Street station.
> *Yes.*
> Is this the first time you've been back?
> *It is.*

Do you recognise it?
Not really.
We're going to visit the place where you first set foot
in England.
The station? Parkeston Quay?

We drive along the twisty lanes that pass through the villages of north Essex. The houses in the village centres have
thatched roofs, timber frames, leaded windows and walls
made from wattle and daub limed in dusted pinks or greys.
As the villages stretch out from their historical centres the
houses change, now facing the road and lining it on either
side. These houses are semi-detached, made with hard bricks
and low-pitched tiled roofs. They have garages built next to
them with painted metal doors. Further out the architecture
changes again. Here the houses are newbuilds, set in small
cul-de-sacs, each house clad in white clapboard made from
MDF or plastic. This plastic clapboard is a recent fashion and
it mimics the architecture of New England, which itself was
built with the memory of the long, timber-clad farm barns
of this area in mind. This is where some of the very first
English settlers of the Americas, the Pilgrim Fathers, came
from, taking their building practices and their architectural
vernacular with them.

We pass through Elmstead Market, Little Bentley, then
past Horsley Cross and onto Tinker Street, the wide road
that broadens into a concrete dual carriageway with control
joints, small gaps in the concrete filled with bitumen.

Then we're in Harwich. We drive through it, its Ha'penny Pier jutting out into the estuary from which fishermen cast their long rods to catch cod, past the house that Samuel Pepys stayed in while he was the MP for Harwich, past the Dockyard which Pepys was in charge of while he was chief secretary to the Admiralty, then down King's Head Street to the house where Christopher Jones was born and lived, the captain and quarter owner of the *Mayflower*.

His house is in a modest terrace and is painted white. We get out of the car to read the information on the wall plaque. As we are reading it a large man leading a small black dog and eating fish and chips walks towards us. He stops and talks to my father while his dog sniffs at my father's feet and calves.

Captain of the *Mayflower* lived there.
Most interesting.
See the plaque?
Yes.
Says it all.

With that the man and his dog leave us. Before he is out of sight my father speaks.

He of all people shouldn't be eating fish and chips.
Why not?
You saw the size of him. He's overweight.
What do you think of the captain of the *Mayflower*'s house?

Scruffy.

The *Mayflower* was built near Harwich.

Was she?

It was originally called the *Mayflower of Harwich*. When it sailed to America most of her crew were from Essex.

Were they?

Before it went to America it spent most of its life sailing between Alicante and Rotherhithe, bringing in Spanish wine, as that was James the first's favourite drink.

I thought she sailed from Plymouth.

It picked up some supplies from there and met another ship, the *Speedwell*, which turned back. But it made the main departure from Rotherhithe.

My father walks back to the car. He turns to face me.

Ships are referred to as 'she', not 'it'.

I know.

So why do you keep saying 'it'?

No good reason.

You never listen, do you?

I don't know.

I must have told you that a thousand times. And another thing.

What?

Before we go to the station.

Yes?

I'd like fish and chips.

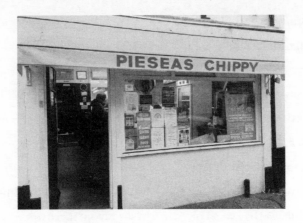

We walk to the Pieseas Chippy on West Street, and order haddock and chips. We walk back up the road to Ha'penny Pier, sit on a bench and eat our fish and chips from their paper wrappers. We overlook the large river basin made by the mouths of two rivers joining, the Orwell and the Stour. The water ripples and gleams. The light is fading. A chilly wind is coming in off the sea. The sky, although darkening, is bright and the clouds are high. Across the bay to our right we can see the port of Felixstowe, which receives ships that are over a quarter of a mile long and where 4 million containers a year are either loaded or unloaded onto the dockside. From this distance the dock cranes look like giant blackbirds pulling worms from the ground as they lift up containers from ships, seemingly with their beaks.

I point over the water to the opposite shore.

Bartholomew Gosnold lived on that side of the estuary at Otley.

24

Who?

Bartholomew Gosnold. He sailed with Walter Raleigh
and then later he pioneered a new sea route in 1602 to
the Americas. He took people with him to start a new
settlement.

Did he?

They only lasted a month and then they came back. His
ship was called *Concord*. It was only 32ft long.

Thirty-two feet?

Yes.

Across the Atlantic?

And then back. Christopher Jones used the sea charts
Gosnold made. The *Mayflower* traced his route. He and
Gosnold probably met near here.

Here?

Yes.

Did you get any tomato sauce?

I hand my father several plastic containers of tomato sauce.
He lays down his chips, opens each packet of sauce and drips
it onto his chips.

*Bloody useless plastic containers. You need to open five to get
a decent amount. Why can't they leave a bloody big bottle out
on the counter like they used to? World's going mad.*

Seagulls start to wheel around on the lookout for
dropped chips.

When Gosnold first arrived near land he cast his nets and they were immediately full of cod and so he named the place Cape Cod.

Did he now?

And a few days later he found an island covered in grapes and he named it after his daughter Martha who was two when she died and he called the place Martha's Vineyard. And she's buried in Bury St Edmunds.

I want to go to the station.

We finish the fish and chips and make the short drive to Harwich International railway station, previously named Parkeston Quay, the site of my father's first steps on British soil. We walk into the station together. Despite its claim to be international it is completely deserted. Four trains pass every hour, one towards and one from London Liverpool Street, plus two local trains. It has two platforms connected by a footbridge. The ferry departs to the Hook of Holland twice a day and, although it is technically a connection between continental Europe and the UK, its claim to internationalism, with all that the word suggests, makes the station's name at least an act of braggadocio, if not deception. We climb the old stairs and cross the bridge to find Platform One, the one for London.

I walked down a gangplank.

And then did you walk across the dockside to the train?

Yes.

Then you would have stood on this platform to go
to London.

Yes, that's right.

So this is where your first steps were. Through this
station and onto this platform.

We stand together. I look at him. He seems unmoved. There's
no reaction from him. No agitation. Not even, it seems, much
interest. His eyes do not flicker. There's no crack in his voice.
His breathing is even. I am holding my breath. My head is
pointing to the ground. I feel a large knot in my stomach. My
head spins slightly. I wonder what's going on.

The platform looks much as it would have when he arrived.
The slabs at the edge of the platform are original, as are the
bricks underneath it that create its structure. Cumbersome
steel features have been added to the station in an attempt to
modernise it, probably in the 1980s, but the original brick is
still clearly visible, as is the large clock. I kneel down and kiss
the platform. When I get up grit from the ground is stuck to
my lips. It tastes bitter and it takes me a while to wipe it off.

What on earth are you doing?

I'm saying thank you to this ground for saving you.

The ground didn't save me. Why do you kiss the ground?

I often kiss the ground. Not sure why. It's something
I've always done since being a child.

Why do you make so much fuss over something that didn't

happen to you?

I wish I knew.

It's odd.

I know it is.

Look over there.

What?

Look.

We walk towards the bell in the shape of a flower.

1.8

My father's unwillingness to talk about his past lasted throughout my childhood and into my twenties, thirties and forties. He simply refused to answer any of my questions about what had happened to him, either in Germany or after his arrival in England. He was more forthright about his twenties, his time in the SAS as their doctor in Malaysia during the communist emergency, where he parachuted into the jungle and was mentioned in dispatches.

He was particularly proud of his role setting up the first doctor's practice to treat the Orang Asli, Malaysia's indigenous people, with his colleague Dr Malcolm Bolton. After leaving the SAS he had helped form part of the 'hearts and minds' operation that provided the Orang Asli with medical treatment. It was part of a policy that allowed them to move out of the disastrous internment camps that the UK government had held them in. His time in Malaysia (then Malaya) meant that our house in Wales had a blowpipe and a quiver of poison-tipped arrows hanging on the living-room wall, which we were instructed to never touch: 'THE POISON ON THEM WILL KILL YOU!'

Once or twice he mentioned his work on the building site of the Festival of Britain, his time at Trinity College

Cambridge, 'which I got into by a complete fluke', as well as his poverty during his student years: 'I lived off Bovril.'

My father looked constantly forwards, constructing his life while gazing steadfastly towards its horizon. He simply refused to look back at his past, even though it haunted him each night. As children we were woken from our sleep by his shouting during his perpetual nightmares. Afterwards we would hear him wandering around the house banging doors, sweeping floors in the small hours, hoovering before dawn, on the landing, outside our bedrooms, dusting, running taps and ceaselessly washing floors with a mop and bucket of water as though these activities could wash his demons away.

His childhood in Germany was left for me to assemble from hints, half-finished stories, blurted-out shards of his history and the memories of others. It took decades to gain some understanding of what had happened to him. Eventually I had to find out in order to try to understand the impact his childhood had had on mine. I needed to understand why I failed at everything, why I achieved nothing, why I refused to speak to people, why I often hated the world, why I lay in bed for days at a time sweating in damp sticky sheets, unable to get up, why I fought and shouted at people, strangers and friends, why I endured long periods of a grey, unfathomable dislike of life, a consistent listlessness, why I refused to eat for days at a time, why a voice inside me for years on end ambushed me at unexpected moments during my daily life, trying to persuade me that I would be better off dead – not in the near future, not tomorrow, but in this moment, now.

2.1

Some mornings during the summer my father would wake us before dawn and take us to Ynyslas, a long ribbon of primrose sand that lies on the western edge of Wales. Ynyslas was a two-hour car ride from Llandrindod, along mountain roads carved into the sides of stone-cropped hills that had signs on them warning drivers of falling rocks. On one side of the road the land curves upwards towards the peaks of hills that catch the sun, their banks covered in gleaming bracken and windswept scrubby oaks. Above them, beyond the tree line, lie sheep-eaten grass and rock. On the other side of the road there are sheer drops.

In those days the mountain roads were narrow and without barriers at their edges and occasionally we would glimpse the wreck of a car far below us, which, having come off the road, had plunged hundreds of feet into the foot of the valley. There it had come to rest and begun to decompose, for a car, having fallen into the valley floor, was impossible to retrieve. Each car's occupants' endings were, as my father cheerfully pointed out, likely to be guaranteed. 'Impossible to survive a crash like that – poor bastards,' he would say as we peered through the car windows. Because my father had only one way of driving, which was, as I had heard a friend of his describe it, 'with his foot flat to the floor', none of us, his children or my mother, particularly wanted to get into the car with him for this journey, partly because his way of dealing with the danger of these mountain roads was to pretend, while approaching a particularly treacherous corner, to lose control of the car.

The mountain road had a white line at its edge, beyond which no car should go, and it was this that my father steered the car towards and then over and where, for a second, he took his hands off the steering wheel as though he hadn't noticed the impending catastrophe. He would then wave his hands towards the windscreen shouting, 'Help! Help! I've lost control of the car!' so that for an instant we would be moving directly towards the edge of the cliff where death awaited us all. At the last moment he would jerk the car away from danger, back onto the correct part of the road, while all of his children – me, my sisters Jane and Sarah, my brothers Simon and David – would scream, my mother beside herself in the front passenger seat, shouting and screaming at his recklessness and sometimes crying, all of which would delight my father who would twinkle with merriment at the emotional outbursts he had caused. Although we were all clearly worried by his behaviour, for him it was the best joke, one that he repeated throughout the journey as well as throughout the years we visited Ynyslas, as though risking the life of his family was a refreshing thing to do. By the time we arrived at the beach of Ynyslas, whose sands stretched for miles around us, the rare intoxicating sight of the sea for us landlocked children laden with stinging air, we were in a state of high anxiety and crying or being sick from the car journey or fighting or, as my father would say, 'being bloody-moody-demanding-spoilt-little-bastards'.

The mountain road to Ynyslas begins in Rhayader, climbs through hills and past reservoirs until it reaches Pont Ar Elan, the tiny stone bridge that crosses the Afon Elan. This is the small stream that was originally the source of the river but is now the source of the Craig Goch reservoir, itself one of several reservoirs that make up the Elan Valley. It is this complex of dams and reservoirs that provides Birmingham with its water: from the edge of Craig Goch an aqueduct travels in a straight line to Birmingham's Frankley Reservoir. Made out of stone and passing through hills and across valleys, this aqueduct was built by Victorian engineers to drop 2ft 4in for every mile it travelled, a slope so subtle that each aqueduct and tunnel appears to the naked eye to be precisely horizontal. Yet this imperceptible slope allows water to flow from Wales into England unassisted and silently. It links the Welsh hills with the industrial factories, the streets and houses of the Midlands city known in Victorian times as the country's forge, providing it with a perpetual supply of clean, soft water.

In order to create the reservoirs the working farms and small villages that populated the Elan Valley were flooded, their inhabitants having been removed under government compulsion. If the summer was extremely hot, the reservoir lowered and began to empty, and remnants of these sunken villages were revealed to us as we drove past. The tips of slate roofs and the edges of stone walls peered out from the water, still standing despite their decades of submergence, the tons of water preserving their structures rather than eroding them. Their presences were ghostly reminders of their former lives, the churches and houses accusatory and skeletal, the wet bones of the villages glaringly full of human absence, caught, it seemed, naked as well as dead. Occasionally, in the local newspaper, photographs of the lost villages were published. One such photograph, taken by a diver, showed the village of Nantgwyllt's old graveyard underwater, the focus of the picture distorted by the light's refractions that take place at such depths, the gravestones leaning at angles among the silt of the reservoir's bed, though clearly defined. In Nantgwyllt the dead were buried first on land before later being drowned and so were unable to be visited by the living.

A Victorian postcard our headmaster Mr Timothy often circulated in class showed the rising water lapping at the foot of the house, the Cwm Elan, before its gradual immersion. There we could see the water creeping up the hillsides after the Elan was dammed. Mr Timothy also told us that if you scrutinise the card you can see two ghostly presences, a face in the trees above the house and the torso of a well-dressed man in the water below it.

It was not long before the Elan Valley was flooded that Percy Shelley stayed in Cwm Elan with his first wife, Harriet Westbrook, the mother of his only living descendants. He was nineteen, she still at school and sixteen when they married. Later he wrote about the Elan Valley: 'Rocks piled on each other to tremendous heights, rivers formed into cataracts by their projections and valleys clothed with woods, present an

appearance of enchantment.' Later Harriet committed suicide
by drowning herself in the Serpentine in Hyde Park, walking
there from Hans Crescent in Knightsbridge where she was
living. She was twenty-one. Percy Shelley had recently left
her to be with Mary Godwin. Her body was found on 10
December 1816. After it had been removed from the water it
was noted that she was pregnant. Her suicide note has been
preserved, her writing an even copperplate, her decision
carefully reasoned, her lines on the paper straight: 'To you my
dear sister I leave all my things as they more properly belong
to you than anyone . . .'

Less than six years later, in July 1822, Shelley also drowned,
in the Gulf of La Spezia near Lerici. He drowned alongside
Edward Williams and Charles Vivien after his boat sank in
a sudden storm that erupted near the coast. He had been to
visit Byron who was staying further up the coast in Livorno
and was returning to see Mary.

Mr Timothy disagreed with the official version of events
and insisted in his flat, unsmiling voice that Shelley had been
murdered. He told us, while holding his cane and repeatedly
tapping it against the side of his leg,

> Shelley's boat was sunk deliberately. An act of illegiti-
> mate piracy. A fisherman made a deathbed confession.
> He told his priest that he had rammed the starboard
> side of Shelley's boat. When they later raised the sunken
> vessel from the seabed, there it was; staved-in on the
> starboard side.

Mr Timothy told us how Shelley's drowned body was washed ashore near Viareggio and cremated on the beach with Byron and his friend Edward Trelawny attending, and how,

> Trelawny saved Shelley's carbonised heart from the iron chamber he was cremated in. And he gave it to Mary Shelley who kept it for the rest of her life. Now his heart is buried in St Peter's churchyard in Bournemouth while his ashes are interred in Rome.

Then we were forced to learn, and recite, Shelley's 'Dirge for the Year', Mr Timothy's bamboo cane hitting our hands if we made a mistake.

> January gray is here,
> Like a sexton by her grave;
> February bears the bier,
> March with grief doth howl and rave,
> And April weeps –

Ynyslas sands are situated north of Aberystwyth in the centre of the bay of Ceredigion, at the mouth of the river. They stretch for miles and are full of high dunes and rare grasses and birds and in summer tiny white flowers. It was there that we would jump from the highest dunes, running across their tops and launching ourselves into the blue air before feeling the sharp pull of gravity gripping our uncontrolled bodies, bringing us back down the steep sides of the dunes into the soft warm sand that always broke our falls however high we jumped. It was there that I learned to jump looking out forwards, waiting for the land to come towards me, rather than me to it, and at the moment of impact allowing my body to go soft as it hit the ground so that it would crumple, 'to spread the force of the fall', as my father kept nagging us to do.

Having hit the ground like a rag doll I could then tumble down the rest of the dune and was never hurt. My ability to fall without injury was thanks to my father teaching us all how to fall as though we were making parachute landings. He had been taught during his SAS basic training, had his parachute wings, and duly passed this knowledge on to his children. He showed us how to bend both knees in one direction and then follow this with a roll while relaxing, urging us never to stiffen up on impact. He had dragged us out after tea one evening and lined us all up on the grass next to Mr Bubyage's path and taught us to fall 'in a controlled way that spreads the shock'. I practised the technique for months and, armed with this confidence, found I could jump from the highest dunes, accelerating up and out as far as I could until I could feel the point at which the forces of acceleration and gravity were in equilibrium for a microsecond, and so stationary, in the air.

2.2

We leave the car park in silence, turn left at a roundabout and enter the docks. Lines of articulated lorries, their signage a compendium of European names – De Haan, Hoyer, CvHeezik, Codognotto, Van Dulja, Schmidt – queue to board the ferry. The orange glow from the sodium floodlights cascades through the night. Enormous cranes dwarf us. The drum of engines vibrates the air.

I drive to the small kiosk for our tickets to be checked. A young, round-faced woman greets us and smiles. 'Ah, the Lichtensteins,' she notes, as she looks down from the height of her kiosk. 'How did you know it was us?' I say. 'From your car number plate,' she replies. 'Do you know all your passengers by name?' I ask. 'Quite a few,' she says. We move forward to passport control. As I hand over both our passports to the serious young man in his blue uniform he says, 'Ah, the Lichtensteins,' and he too looks down from his kiosk and he too smiles and says, 'Have a great trip.' We drive across the docks and up a spiral metal road shaped like a helter-skelter, over a clanking metal bridge that joins the ship to the land, then through the *Stena Britannica*'s mouth and into its belly. My father bites his nails as we are inched close to the cars in front of us with much shouting and gesticulation by men in orange boiler suits, despite there being hardly any other cars on the deck. It's midweek in November and freezing. Not many people are making the trip tonight.

We take our bags from the car. 'I'll take your case if you like,' I say to my father. 'I can manage perfectly well, thank you,' he replies as he lifts it out of the car. Looking tired but defiant, his back hunched over, his head towards the ground, he walks across the steel car deck into the lobby area, then into the lift that takes us up to our cabin. As we get out of the lift we are greeted with a smile from one of the cabin crew: 'Welcome aboard.' We settle into the cabin that has two beds next to a porthole. They're close to each other and I realise, as does he, that we have not slept in the same room for over half a century.

> I think that you stayed with an American family when you first arrived in England.
> *That's right. I stayed with an American family for a few weeks.*
> And then they went back?
> *That's correct. They went back to America leaving me on my own.*
> How strange. Who were they?
> *I've absolutely no idea.*
> How strange.
> *I got sent to Hastings and lived there on my own in a flat. When I first arrived I went swimming in the sea and stupidly left my belongings on the beach. When I came back my father's watch and the carpet my mother had given me had been stolen.*

What happened then?

I was collected and taken to a boarding school. Someone paid for me. I don't know who. I never did find out. No one would tell me. Even years later I tried to find out but no one would let on. I assumed it was the American family.

Someone paid your fees?

Yes.

All the way through your schooling?

Yes.

Amazing.

Luck.

My father lies down on the bed's white sheets and gazes through the porthole towards the lights onshore. Together we watch the ship's docking ropes being untied from the quay and winched onto the ship and as it casts its moorings we float into the estuary. Harwich, the first place he saw on his arrival, twinkles and recedes. The diesel engines of the ship vibrate us gently. My father falls asleep, head to one side. In the middle of the night he wakes me, prodding me hard on my arm.

Where am I?

We're on a boat.

Are we going to Paris?

No, no, to Berlin. Remember?

I need to see the bursar.

Later. Tomorrow.

I need to change some money.

Dad. You've had a dream. We're driving to Berlin,
remember?
Not Paris?
Not Paris. Berlin.

He gets back into his bed. His face is contorted. He draws his
duvet over him. I watch him for some time. His skin is grey.
His knuckles are blue. He quivers a little and then falls asleep.

2.3

One day when I was eight years old and playing in the front garden during the school's summer holidays I noticed a woman on the other side of Pentrosfa looking towards our garden. She was holding a small, dark-blue suitcase and smoking a cigarette. After a while she crossed the road and stood at our front gate and watched me. She was in her forties, small, agile and dark-haired, unsmiling and with a direct gaze. She wore no make-up and was dressed in jeans and a plain navy-blue jumper with a scarf. She lit a new cigarette as soon as the one she was smoking came to an end, stubbing it out on the lid of the cigarette carton. Her index and first fingers were yellow with tar. From the gate she spoke to me in a low voice, with an accent that was so pronounced I could hardly understand her.

'Your father? Here?'
He's at work.
'Doctor? Yes?'
Yes.
'His house?'
Yes.
'Yonathan?'
What?

'Jonathan?'

Yes

'I am Toni.'

Tony?

'Your aunt. The sister of your father.'

At this point I didn't know what to do so I went into the house to fetch my mother, who came out into the front garden and walked to the front gate.

'I am Toni.'

'Hans's sister?'

'Yes.'

'How extraordinary.'

'It is a surprise?'

'Yes it is. Please, you'd better come in. Have you come far?'

'Israel.'

Toni, smoking continuously, walked up Mr Bubyage's path towards the house until, at the front door, my mother stopped her.

'I'm sorry but you'll have to put your cigarette out. Hans doesn't tolerate smoking in the house.'

'I'm his sister.'

'He really does insist that no one smokes indoors.'

'His older sister.'

And with that Toni pushed past my mother and walked through the front door into our house holding her cigarette, which was still alight. She strode down the small tiled hall into the kitchen, sat down on a chair next to the stove and blew smoke rings up to the ceiling.

She stayed with us for two weeks and was uncannily quiet throughout the day, speaking very little to anyone and almost nothing to us children, though she observed us intently. After we went to bed she became far from quiet. We could hear her in intense conversation with my father late into the night, both of them speaking German, the unfamiliar rhythm and sounds of this strange, apparently fraught language thickening the air, its inflexions distancing my father from us as his original language gripped his tongue. I had never heard German spoken before; he refused to speak it at home. For him, it remained the language of oppression, and when he spoke it was as though he distanced himself from himself.

In the morning both my parents and Toni looked tired and washed-out. Despite my father's pleas she insisted on smoking in the house. He deferred, so Toni became the only person who was ever allowed to smoke indoors. Once I asked my father,

> What are you talking to her about in the evening?
> *Nothing.*
> You talk a lot.
> *Be quiet.*

Toni continued to speak very little to us during the day but each night she spoke volumes to my father and I could see, as we all could, that he was becoming drained by her.

As it was summertime she came to Ynyslas with us, sitting in the back of the car continually smoking so that we could hardly breathe. When we climbed past the reservoirs she noted their beauty and grandeur, not verbally, but silently, her dark eyes drinking in the sparse landscape, her head turning gently as we drove past the waters, her cigarette held quietly, the ash floating into clouds before settling on the car seats as we passed the dams with their towers and sloping stone. At times she closed her eyes slowly, her lids gliding over her corneas as though she was checking her body's presence, astonished that she was with her younger brother, a survivor's dream. Oddly she did not find the mountain road dangerous but instead seemed to relax, watching the views across the reservoirs through the car window, pulling them, it seemed, inside herself with tremendous concentration as though she wanted to fill something up. Even when my father took his hands off the steering wheel and shouted she just laughed at him and, instead of being frightened, tried to pronounce the names of the villages we passed through – Cwmystwyth, Pont-rhyd-y-groes, Abermagwr and Rhydyfelin.

When we arrived at the sands I walked with her in silence down to the sea's edge. I showed her the dunes and stood with her as she skilfully lit her cigarettes in the wind. We climbed to the top of the highest dune and stood together watching the view out to sea, the breakers crashing far out on a sandbar before gently rippling across the shallows, spreading a wide, thin layer of bubbling water across the smooth sand. It was there that she turned to me and I noticed her eyes were very like my father's, an unusually bright, almost forget-me-not blue. She said,

> If you dream long enough and if you have patience you
> can have anything.

I was surprised to hear her speak a full sentence and didn't know what to say to this strange statement. So I just smiled nervously and stood leaning against the wind, the sole of one of my bare feet placed on top of the other. I had no idea what she was talking about, but I knew she was trying to reach me, extending something towards me. But what it was I did not know. Drawing on her cigarette she repeated,

> You must have patience.

Not knowing how to reply, and sensing a weight upon me to do something, I showed her how to make a correct parachute landing and encouraged her to jump off the top of the dune with me. Because the dunes were perhaps 20 or 30ft high she laughingly refused and so I showed her my trick of running and then hurling myself high into the air. After landing in a flurry of sand and coming to rest I turned to look up at her to see her on the dune's summit, her hair blowing, her cigarette burning, the sun high in the sky, her gaze away from me and towards the sea. She was unimpressed, it seemed, with what I considered one of the major accomplishments of my life.

She remained entirely silent during the drive home. She seemed more or less to inhabit her own world, absorbed by something beyond the reach of us, my aunt, whom I saw many times during this two-week period of my life, but never again.

2.4

I wake abruptly, mouth dry from the air conditioning, to see, across the gap that lies between us, my father. He's asleep, flat on his back, chin up, skin sallow, tips of his toes pointing towards the underside of the blue serge mattress of the top bunk that lies above him. The ship's white cotton duvet has tented over him so that his feet stick out from underneath; chipped lemon-yellow nails, weird, protruding-too-far-out ankle bones shared by both of us, mouth open, large chest as tight as a drum, lower teeth bent, chipped. I scrutinise him, lean on my elbow and look at him calmly, watching him as he sleeps, a forensic gaze. He's shrunk, his hair thinned and white, skin falling away at the elbows, jaw muscles as tense as stone, enlarged, rigid neck muscles, faded pockmarks on his upper cheek, skin sun-damaged where it tightens across the edges of his skull, quivering Adam's apple at the top of his standing-up-and-out windpipe, soles of his feet the colour of dark gold wax. What was I frightened of? I turn to the sea. Through the thick, double-glazed porthole the waves are far below. In silence dawn's light skids across the water, bounced, refracted, bent, pirouetting; volumes of it poured onto each wave and fleck.

The *Stena Britannica*'s diesel engines pulse 120ft below us; unfeasible mechanical giants, four of them, eleven decks down, each one screwed to the ship's hull. They are designed in the same way as a car engine but scaled up massively and, joined together, produce 49,080 horsepower. I try to imagine the sight of the equivalent number of horses in front of the ship, pulling us along, against currents, past buoys, along shipping lanes, through the astonished water, their speed scintillating as they gallop, their numbers surprising even to each other, thrilled and stretching as far as the eye can see, horses of all colours and sizes – pit ponies and drays, piebalds and shires and Suffolk punches, geldings and stallions and mares, their odd-toed ungulate hooves hitting the water, their traces made of leather, linking each other, square miles of horses joined and straining the rope that pulls this ship that is the size of a large village with all its food and traffic, a town of horses, a sea of them, eating oats and grass and shitting their urine-coloured shit.

He wakes, lifts his head minutely, raises it from the pillow. I watch his eyes as consciousness returns to him, flickering in and out for a short time. I watch his surprise as he transitions into the world. Without speaking he lies for some time staring upwards and then wordlessly slips out of bed in his white Y-fronts, dark hairs covering his back, large indentations down both of his thighs, craters left from boils from when he was a child. When we were children he used to smile at us as he pointed to them, pleased, almost giggling, each dent in his leg a story. Now they gleam in the cabin's light, flecks of albino, the scars' lack of pigmentation spatterings of skin from another time, the history of Europe embossed on him.

In the cabin he walks with tremendous care, his hands slightly outstretched in front of him, his feet turned in, towards the shower at the back of the room with its smell of bleach and cleaning liquid. I hear the taps turn on and the toilet flush. Then he's back out and sitting on the bed, wet, water dripping off him. I'd forgotten about his habit of never drying himself with a towel after a bath or shower but insisting on getting dressed while still wet. He sits wrapped in his towel, tied with a knot like a sarong around his waist, and slowly takes his clothes out of his giant suitcase – beige cotton socks that take an age to put on as he carefully aims his feet into them, smart plaid shirt that sticks to him because his skin is still wet, hand-crafted cufflinks threaded through double shirt cuffs with tottery exactitude and immense absorption, faded dark-green moleskin trousers from Ede & Ravenscroft, sent to him by post and properly pressed, brown polished shoes, shining from some of his spit mixed with polish – a military habit. It is the casual wardrobe of a fictional Englishman who belongs to a certain class and is a certain age. For him this is a meticulous costume and these are the garments of disguise. They throw people off the scent, a shield of clothes, sartorial armour, a deflection of attention from his history of immigration and loss. He is silent. I tell him about the power of the diesel engines, sharing statistics with him as he always did with me when I was a child.

Forty-nine thousand and eighty horsepower.
Really?

Can you imagine what all those horses would look like
if they were pulling the ship together?
What are you talking about?

I plough on. I don't know why. There's something in me
that will not stop, pushing me through the awkwardness of
his lack of interest, my voice slightly distant to me, nervous,
tired, a bit shrill, the creep of my intruding self-consciousness
making my mind race, quietly mocking my attempt at communication, knowing it's misjudged but seemingly unable to
do anything about it. My deference to him is still present. I
am still weak in his presence.

Guess how many tons the propellers weigh?
I don't know.
There are two of them. Guess.
I really don't care.
They weigh 22 tons each and this ferry weighs 64,000.
How do you know?
I looked it up before I came.

Now he's clearing his throat. Eyes cast down. Tight lips.
Nearly dressed. Sitting on the edge of the bed.

Very dry air in here.
It's the air conditioning.
Throat's sore. Let's get some coffee.
It's going to be a long drive.

Obviously.

It's 600 miles from the Hook of Holland to Berlin.

Six hundred?

Then back again. Will you be okay?

How do I know?

Do you remember that VW Passat you had?

Yes I do.

Black-and-white checked seats.

Very comfortable. Would have been perfect for this drive.

2.5

I'm sixteen and I'm standing next to my younger brother Simon who is twelve and so ill he is as thin as a matchstick. Simon is tall for his age, and skeletal, the deepest, blackest, charcoal rings under both of his brown pumpkin eyes that protrude from his skull, cruel eczema breaking out all over his body, itchy, itchy skin, scratch-scratch-scratch. 'Stop scratching! Stop scratching!' Small bubbles of blood stand out on the darkening inside cusps of each elbow, white dust of dead skin on his cheeks, his frame of bones clearly visible, his perpetual illness a constant background to our child-hoods. His visits to doctors are a continual occurrence. His dry breath catches in his oesophagus, his lotions and potions and creams and special shampoos and asthma medication and pills of myriad colours clutter the bathroom. It's been going on since his arrival from hospital where he was delayed after his birth due to 'complications' and breathing difficulties. We are standing next to my father who in turn is standing next to the brand-new diesel VW Passat that he's just collected. It has black-and-white checked cloth seats and 'Stargaze' silver alloy wheels. 'Worth the extra money for the benefits in road-holding alone,' he claims, as though he's learned the car brochure off by heart.

Can you believe it, 50 miles to the gallon, can you believe
that, unbelievable!

The Minis were left behind some years ago, the Land Rovers
have been sold, the infatuation with ancient, cheap, second-
hand small Renaults has also passed and now this car has
arrived: finally, a very-normal-brand-new-very-respectable
car for the first time. Except for one thing – it's a VW.

You always said you could never buy a VW.
I did.
So why've you changed your mind?
It's a very good-looking car.
But you said you hated them.
Just shut up.

He marches off. A memory. A disturbance. I shouldn't have
unearthed it, whatever it is. I can guess at it but never know.
Then he's back. Catch pulled, bonnet opened, bonnet heaved
up on self-supporting hydraulic struts.

Can you believe it? Hydraulic struts for a bonnet! They keep
it up on its own!

He leans far into the engine bay, half his body under the
bonnet, cobalt-blue wool tie shaking around, arms waving,
showing Simon and me the fuel pump and the fuel line and
'the injectors that spray the diesel into the cylinders as the

pistons compress the air'. He points in different directions at once. 'This is the water-pump belt, this is the power-steering belt, this is the air intake.' I see his bitten nails, not bitten down towards the quick from his fingertips, but bitten from the front inwards towards the flesh of each finger, chewed over and over, tiny pieces bitten off and spat out or eaten, until each nail bleeds so that all of them, though they are the same size as normal nails, are cratered and pitted and twinkle in the dark light under the car's bonnet. I notice them close up as my head dips into the engine bay too. They're the same colour they've always been – straw and urine with hints of saffron and blood. They're a disturbed knurling of fingernails, a Daliesque dream, a Pieter Bruegel the Elder detail, a Louise Bourgeois exhibit in *The Return of the Repressed*. They would blend in next to her giant welded spiders and her dark tableaux of oppression. They would be titled 'The Nails of Extremely Difficult Suffering'. They are the dark opposite of a nail bar's promise – a manicurist's worst nightmare.

> *Never, ever start to bite your nails! Promise me that! Look what happened to me! I can't ever stop! Look at them!*

He often shouts this instruction out at mealtimes at the kitchen table while holding his hands up, his fingernails facing us all, exhibit 'A' in a police investigation into fingernail torture. My father continues.

Diesels detonate spontaneously under pressure whereas petrol engines need a spark to detonate.

I look at the incomprehensible tangle of pipes and tubes in the engine bay and say nothing. It's all a total confusion to me. Simon might be ill and flirting with death but he's far quicker than I am, despite the fact that I'm nearly five years older. He carries on.

So, Dad, that means if you mix diesel vapour and air together it explodes on its own?
Only if you compress it down to one-twentieth of its original volume.
The pressure makes it explode?
Compressed air heats up. Get it down to one-twentieth of its original volume and it heats up enough to make the added diesel vapour spontaneously combust. That's why diesel engines have a compression ratio of twenty to one.
Is that why diesels don't have spark plugs?
Exactly.

Bonnet slammed down, car door opened. My father throws himself inside, making the seat springs earn their living, in his tweed jacket the colours of autumnal leaf flecked with threads of mustard, and his mahogany polished shoes sent to him in the post by a shoemaker from somewhere in the country on a set date every summer; none of us knows where because he'll never tell anybody – 'Cost a small bloody fortune – only shoes that will fit me – twenty-six bones in each foot – can't afford to get anything wrong in that department!' They're the only type of shoe he will wear and he refuses to throw his old ones away, 'Just-in-case-I-need-them.' The consequence is that there are always at least nine or ten pairs in the house at any one time, each in gradated degrees of erosion. They range from the brand-new, unmarked 'best' pair worn for parties, official functions and funerals, down to the oldest pair, over ten years old, forlorn, curling tongue, flapping sole half disintegrated, no laces, resoled by the cobbler many times and now used for gardening. His shoes are a living illustration of the journey from just after shoe birth to just before shoe death, the complete shoe life, all stages of the journey represented, all lined up in a row on a shelf in the cupboard under the stairs. Most are polished daily with Kiwi shoe polish and two horsehair-bristle shoe brushes, 'one to put it on, one to take it off', front, back and sides, as well as underneath them, between the front sole and the heel. 'That's how you can tell if a pair of shoes has been properly polished.'

He turns the key, slams the door, winds the window down, revs the engine (82 horsepower), wheels spinning for a fraction of a second on the gravel, spitting chippings from the tyres, off to do something important/can't stay here chatting all day/promised to see Mr Jones about his pneumonia/give blood/go hang-gliding/anaesthetise someone for a hernia in the cottage hospital/go to surgery/pick up muesli from Van's wholefood shop – 'Isn't he a marvellous businessman to make a shop like that work in such a small town? Just goes to show what someone with enterprise can do.'

After he's gone my brother and I fall back into our own worlds. There's no talk between us. There's nothing to say as the cloud of dust begins to settle from the stirred-up chippings outside our house. My father's energy is so white-hot and livid that after he's left I realise I've been holding my breath, unable to suck in the appropriate amount of oxygen to stop my brain spinning as it always does. I'm frightened but also exhilarated and more alive on the fragile edge of his storms, like light hitting water, a cascade of life. His car engine revs in the distance, pushed to breaking point, the engine straining, the tyres only just holding their grip on the black tarmac, the sounds of the new car fading as he disappears, the songs of birds now heard in his absence, thrushes and sparrows, pigeons, wind through bushes, cool air on our faces. We go our separate ways in silence, my emaciated brother and I, him to his bedroom plastered from head to foot with pictures of aircraft – planes, helicopters and gyrocopters, jets, turboprops, experimental home-made planes, constructed of plywood or balsawood or copper or any other ridiculously unsuitable material, their landing gear made from wheelbarrow wheels, 'with pneumatic tyres of course', my brother tells me quite seriously, 'to help create a smooth landing'.

And me off out. Anywhere will do. But out – in all weathers, outside, into the air, alone, far away, along the lanes, tasting the oxygen, in–out, in–out, my chest heaving, out past the hedges, feeling my pulse through the curves of my neck. Then out past the sprays of crisp white hawthorn in spring, masses arriving suddenly, unexpectedly, and each year there again and a blessing, yet almost-dead dark-grey branches in winter, and soaked in the occluded light. Then out further, feet certain, hitting the ground into the rippling hills with their silence and their acceptance, on my own, and further, across the hillocks, jumping, tripping, falling over, rolling, springy turf flexing my feet, pushing up through bracken, past the tree line, over rocks, up towards the top of the hill, untrammelled by the not-so-subtle spot tests about the inner secrets of the bloody fucking internal combustion engine, either petrol or diesel.

2.6

Isolation and loneliness are strange comrades and came upon me at first gradually and then very quickly. After I finished school and because I had somehow managed to fail nearly all my exams, I took a job as a farm labourer in Bedfordshire where I lived on my own in a small caravan with a golden-yellow ceiling. The caravan was boiling in summer and freezing in winter. During winter I slept in a sleeping bag with all my clothes on and with spare coats resting on top of me. In the morning I broke the ice in the washing-up bowl in the caravan's sink. As I had no friends or family nearby and much of the work was done alone, I began to withdraw, to find it difficult to talk to people, my jaw muscles seeming to atrophy due to their lack of use.

The caravan was old and had no toilet or shower and so I was allowed to use the ones in the farmhouse. I was also provided with a meal every evening after everyone else in the farmer's family had eaten. I would sit in the back kitchen and eat alone and then walk back, in winter, in the pitch-black through fields to the caravan. Initially I found the farm work enjoyable and peaceful. My colleagues Mr Laird and Cyril Serjeant kept an eye on me. Mr Laird had a pacemaker, a hernia, was diabetic and was blind in one eye. He taught me to be patient, to slow down, showed me how to hammer a nail, to saw wood carefully, how to use a sledgehammer, to put up a gatepost, herd sheep, make friends with cattle before moving them, to concrete the base of a silo, to fix the gearbox of a Massey Ferguson tractor, all in a kind of silence.

One evening, while eating my meal in the farmhouse, I read in the *Evening Post and Echo* the main news story of the day. It was about a man who had murdered his wife with a knitting needle. He was now on the run and the front page warned the public that he remained in the area and that on no account was he to be approached. That night I was woken by a pushing on my caravan's door. Fearing that the knitting needle murderer was about to break in, I froze. The pushing carried on and on and then the door handle turned. I had previously had a job painting a helicopter hangar in Sumburgh, in the Shetlands, where I worked with a man who beat people up for money. He had told me that if you wanted to hurt someone in the night you should blind your victim, preferably with car headlights, before hitting them. That way they couldn't see you. Bearing this in mind I moved my hand imperceptibly to find my torch. I decided to push open the caravan window that was next to my bed, shine the torch in the murderer's face and then run. I waited until the caravan door was pushed again and then I flung open the caravan window. But instead of opening the window, I put my arm straight through it, shattering the glass. The noise filled my ears, my shining torch lighting the dark fields around me, the shards of broken glass glinting on the ground below, my hand and arm bleeding from the cuts made by the small pieces of glass sticking out of them. There was no murderer. A few sheep had been at the door. I watched them run away from me. My body was soaked in the sweat that arrives with extreme fear. As I picked shards of glass out of my forearm and my wrist, watching my now flowing blood streak my skin in the dark, I knew that something had gone wrong with me, that something deep within me was broken, but what it was I could not tell or reach, for I had no kind of language to communicate it to myself.

2.7

We leave our cabin, walk along the ship's windowless
interior, past a sign that directs us up a set of steps to the
'Lounge-Restaurant'. Each step has fluted lights at its base
and is laid with strips of parrot-blue carpet. As we climb the
stairs we pass a door with a sign that says 'Truckers' Café',
and in smaller print, 'Truckers Only'. It is through this that
my father glimpses one of his favourite things – a cooked
breakfast.

> *Did you see in there?*
> I did.
> *A cooked breakfast.*
> I know.
> *The full English.*
> I saw.
> *Let's go in.*

He is suddenly effervescent. I say,

> We're not allowed to.
> *Why not?*
> Because we're not driving an HGV. The café is called

'Truckers' Café' because it's for truckers.

Truckers. What a contemptible word. Truckers. What does it actually mean? The word is simply wrong. An Americanism, I suppose.

Words gain acceptance through usage. It's a very flexible thing, the English language. There's no such thing as a rigid, stable language; meaning is constantly fluctuating . . .

I hear my voice in its pious and educational mode emanating from me and so trail off mid-sentence due to a sudden loss of confidence. I fall into a kind of silence that often comes upon me and which, because I don't know how to get out of it, even after all these years, builds to become a loaded, fraught Pinteresque pause. And so we stand hovering at the entrance to the Truckers' Café in silence, two Beckettian characters pinned to a carpet – Pozzo and Lucky.

There's bacon, eggs, sausage, black pudding, fried bread and tomatoes.

His eyes crease with happiness.

We're not allowed in there, it's for the lorry drivers.
And who's going to care?

I see a force comes up from inside him, solidifying him, making him more upright, the edges of his torso more clearly defined against the background of the ship's décor. He is marshalling the power of his internal world. He's decided he's going into the Truckers' Café whether we're allowed to or not. I say,

> It would make me too uncomfortable.
> *Bollocks.*
> Sitting in there.
> *Who cares?*
> Thinking they'll ask us to leave at any moment.
> *Why do you worry so much?*

My father strides in through the doors of the Truckers' Café, pushing with surprising strength at the double swing doors that open quickly. It's as though he's the sheriff in a western. I trail behind him so that as one of the doors swings back towards me it hits my right shoulder, knocking me slightly off balance. I'm in an alternative film to the western he is starring in. It runs almost simultaneously, it uses the same sets, it even runs at the same speed. Except I'm starring in a tragi-comedy about crippling insecurity and how things never quite work out.

He picks up a tray, wipes it with his sleeve in a flamboyant display of hygiene awareness and then slides it along the chrome rails of the counter towards the cooked breakfast. I follow him towards the individually lit stoneware bowls of fried mushrooms, bacon, black pudding, fried bread and eggs. Lorry drivers are sitting, quietly reading. A TV is on in the background. Its flickering tape of red at the bottom of the screen makes announcements in English while the presenter reads the news in Dutch. I hear a voice behind me.

> *Do you have an HGV ticket?*
> No, we don't.
> *Then you can't eat in here, this is the Truckers' Café.*
> Of course.

I look up at a tall, dignified Dutchman in his late fifties dressed in a black uniform. He speaks quietly, patiently.

> The Lounge-Restaurant for the general public is up the
> stairs on the next deck.
> *What's that?*

says my father loudly, suddenly clinging to his tray as though it's one of the most valuable possessions he's ever owned. The man repeats himself.

> This café is for the truckers.
> *What bloody nonsense.*

I see my father's body expand, his spine stretch, his breath deepen.

> *What's a bloody trucker, anyway?*
> It's someone who drives an HGV vehicle.

It rhymes with fucker.

Yes, it does.

Well, really, this is all totally unacceptable. Why you can't use the Queen's English is beyond me.

The public buy their breakfasts from the Lounge-Restaurant.

You've already told us that.

It's located up the next flight of stairs on the right-hand side on deck ten. There's a lift if you need it.

I don't need a bloody lift, thank you very much. I'm perfectly capable of taking the stairs.

Of course, sir.

Totally unhealthy bloody contraptions, lifts.

Dad, come on.

My father looks at me and then at the tall man in his pressed uniform.

I'm going to write to the management and complain.

About what?

About the fact that I'm not allowed in the Truckers' Café.

No one would mind if you did that, sir.

The man replies without any hint of aggression, a kind smile crossing his face, his hazel, lidded eyes partially hidden behind the reflections of his steel-wire spectacle frames, weary creases over his eyebrows caused by having to sustain the pressures of providing an 'outstanding customer experience' to people like my father. On the landing we linger for a moment. 'Worth a try,' says my father, an almost youthful spring in his step, colour having now entered the spidery capillaries of his cheeks. We climb another flight of steps, him speedier now, leg muscles working, blood pumping, adrenaline flowing, the tension during the encounter in the Truckers' Café for him a life-enhancing tonic.

Then, just before the entrance to the Lounge-Restaurant we pass two enormous electrical massage chairs. My father stops and gazes at them. 'Look at those,' he says, as though they are the rarest animals from the savannah. 'Massage chairs.' He peers at the advertising copy that has been printed in magenta and violet inks and is written in bubble font. After a second, as though he is a sage passing on profound knowledge to the waiting masses, he reads, 'These chairs promise to deliver.' He stops, clears his throat and, lowering his voice by a semitone, proclaims, 'These chairs *promise* to deliver a zero-gravity massage; 3D body care for your whole body.' People pass us on the stairs, groups of families and friends, some fully dressed, others in pyjamas. A small girl holding a large stuffed giraffe with a damaged neck makes her way slowly up the stairs. Two boys dressed in superhero costumes chase past, one with long red hair, the other brown. Both hold large toy diggers. 'What-bloody-dreadful-syntax-who-ever-wrote-this-bloody-bilge-should-be-shot,' says my father loudly, his eyes narrowed, an air of blinkered concentration stiffening him.

These chairs *promise* to target the areas that need a firm, relaxing massage instead of blindly hitting areas inches away from your trouble spots.

He stops and turns to me and says: 'I'll have a go. Sounds convincing. Costs four pounds. Do you have four pounds?'

The chairs are covered in thin streaks of sweat and dead skin cells. A faint odour emanates from them. It's six in the morning. I say,

> Four pounds?
> *In coins.*
> In coins?
> *Obviously.*
> Yes, I do.

With a leap my father throws himself onto the nearest chair. It is so large it seems to miniaturise him, his legs and arms suddenly tiny when set against the mass of black padded vinyl. I'm sure both chairs are giving off an atmosphere of restrained violence until I realise that it has nothing to do with them. It's my own inner feelings of repressed anger. I am projecting my own violence onto a pair of black vinyl massage chairs. This is due to the painfully familiar situation I'm now in – humouring my father, deferring to him while acting as his helper. I feel like I'm from the social services. Or that I've been given a community sentence. By the local magistrate. I am serving a punishment for a minor crime.

I place the coins through a silver metal slot on the arm of the chair. Each pound tumbles through a series of mechanical levers. They make a '*ting*' sound as they hit the bottom of the collecting box. The sounds are reassuring, a reminder of the reliability of gravity. As I insert the last coin I stand back quickly, wondering what will happen. But nothing happens. The chair remains inert. Enraged my father bangs it with his fists then with both his legs. He gets off it, stands next to it and kicks it. I say,

> It's broken.
> *That just cost four pounds.*
> Let's go and eat.
> *Really.*
> Look – I need coffee. Do you need a coffee?
> *All right.*

We carry on up the stairs, push through another set of wooden double doors and enter the Lounge-Restaurant. It's not quite 6.15 a.m. and I'm exhausted and I have become what I become when I'm with my father. An emotional and physical wreck.

2.8

My mother hated Mr Bubyage's path. To her it was linear and grey and intrusive and out of scale with the small lawn it had been laid across and therefore it was unkind and it ruined the look of the garden. She had wanted a path of stepping stones made from Welsh slate, not concrete. She and my father had argued about it for weeks and so when the path was laid she saddened a small part further, withdrawing into herself a particle at a time while her children watched. And so it was that when we returned from a long journey in the red Mini and parked next to the black wooden front gate of the house she would look up at the path and exhale a long sigh.

We all understood why my mother, a beautiful and generous woman, was sad. It was because my sister Ruth had died. I often saw my mother weeping, sitting next to a picture of Ruth. She had died in her carrycot in the back of the car – a cot death. At that time my father had a two-seater MG. Jane and I were in the front with my mother, on the way home from seeing relatives, when we stopped in a lay-by surrounded by tall pine trees. It was evening. My mother screamed and screamed. It was years later that my father told me what had happened.

We went to see Beryl's brother George. Ruth was in a carrycot in the back of the car. While we were driving home I put my hand behind me to check if she was all right and I realised she was cold. I stopped the car in a lay-by and lifted her out but she was already dead. She had died in the car.

How terrible for you.

I wouldn't put a baby in a place like that now. We know more about cot deaths these days.

My father went back to work the day after Ruth died. I was two and a half years old and my sister Jane was fourteen months old. Although it was insisted later that I didn't know anything about it or remember it, I did remember it. I remembered it because I had heard my mother's scream, a scream that cannot be forgotten – and much later I would hear the same scream again.

2.9

The Lounge-Restaurant is a large welcoming space. Its ceiling is high and it stretches across the width of the ship. Large portholes sit on either side of it and to its front are large windows that form a wall of glass through which we see the horizon and dawn's light. Around us is the traffic of the North Sea: a surprising number of ships and boats, many close to us, all with their lights on, red for port, green for starboard. We sit down on padded canary-yellow armchairs next to a Formica-topped table. The material covering the chairs reflects yellow light on our skin, casting us with a jaundiced tinge. 'I'm very hungry,' declares my father. 'Very hungry, starving, totally famished.' 'I'll get some breakfast,' I answer, and head towards the breakfast bar of the Lounge-Restaurant. I choose scrambled eggs, fried bread, mushrooms, tomatoes, toast, slices of salami, different kinds of cheese, croissants, small plastic packets of marmalade and mugs of coffee. I need two journeys to carry it all, bringing each load on a large brown tray. We eat in silence. The sun rises beside us, pours more of dawn's light upon the water. Some of the tips of the waves look incandescent.

The ship moves towards the coast. We enter the complex of waterways that have been built around the effluents of the

Rhine. Stretching out as far as the eye can see are harbours, jetties and quays, ships, cranes and containers. The Hook of Holland is on our left and a man-made island full of docks and canals is on our right. Land and water are intricately laced together. There's so much light it's like a skin – thick lashings of it, a chiaroscuro around all objects and people, a cornucopia, the sea's surface alive.

The waterways are thronged with boats; tugs pulling long lines of rusting brick-red barges heaped full of stones and earth with diggers perched on their top at leery angles, the captains at their wheels, nonchalant, leaning against low metal doors, their windows open, one hand on the ship's wheel. Sailors at the stern, almost level with the water, which sloshes over the decks and around their feet. The weight of their bodies is set low inside them, held in their feet and calves, their soles planted on the slippery wood of the tugs' rear decks, legs set apart, short, tan riggers' boots, toes curled tight in steel toe-caps; an Avercamp of activity.

In the distance rows of ships are being unloaded by cranes, the brothers and sisters of those at Felixstowe. Their containers are lifted onto the docks and then moved by smaller, double-beamed 'ship to shore' cranes, where they're spread out and stacked high. Each is loaded onto a lorry that queues to receive them individually, each container salt-faded, brine-green, pearl-blue, rust-brown, and holding goods from all over the world. Then they set off out along the roads of Rotterdam, the largest port in western Europe.

It's not just the light, or the shape of the land that is so surprising. It's not even the industrious, beehive-like activity. It's the scale of the imposition made by man onto the land and into the sea that is startling. Everything has been altered and remade for the benefit of shipping. Seabeds have been dug out, channels deepened, acres of land reclaimed, artificial lakes created, the flow of rivers altered, huge dams constructed and hundreds of miles of dykes built. It is the result not just of huge activity but also of an audacity of thinking. The area has been built up year by year, over centuries, starting with the smallest reclamation of land from the sea, until it became a country, the Netherlands, half of it no more than 3ft above sea level and a quarter of it below. A sunken country imagined into being.

Incredible isn't it?

The breakfast?

The docks. Do you remember any of this?

Not really.

What was it like when you came through it on the *Kindertransport?*

The ships were much smaller then. And hundreds of men on the docks moving goods around. Before containers arrived.

Did people wave at you as you boarded the ship?

No.

The pictures of the *Kindertransport* often show adults waving at them supportively.

No one took much notice of us.

That's surprising.

Not really.

Do you remember anything else?

I do remember there were thousands of bikes and at one point
there was a traffic jam of them. I remember a policeman had
to control them. And everyone had to stand for ages with
one of their legs on one of their pedals, the other stretched
out onto the ground.

He picks up his coffee and looks at it closely.

You know they effectively stole money off us?
The Nazis?
The massage chairs.
It doesn't matter.
I'm going to complain.
It's only four pounds.
It's the principle.

The remains of the coffee sit in the bottom of the cups – cold,
brown grounds. The saucers are startling white discs on the
marble-patterned Formica table. Our breakfast plates have
been scraped, leaving streaks of orange egg yolk and tomato
sauce. The two oblong brown trays with their lipped edges
are stacked together and rest on the floor. On the plates the
cutlery is set together, the forks turned up, the knives laid
down upon their sides, the teaspoons are at rest on the table.
Outside great black-backed gulls circle in the air, the strength
of their wings impossible, their blunt yellow beaks curved
down at the ends. And so present and full is this moment of

the everyday that I finally ask the question that has taken years
to constellate itself inside me.

The other children on the *Kindertransport*?
What about them?
What were they doing? Photographs show them playing
violins or in happy little knots comforting each other.
Not on my train.
. . .
They wept.
. . .
For the whole journey.
. . .
Tremendous grief.
. . .
I didn't cry.
. . .
At the border of Germany the Nazi guards left the train.
. . .
I opened the window. Watched the countryside pass.
. . .
My mother told me that I was going away for a holiday.
. . .
That I'd be returning home in a few weeks.
. . .
And I'd believed her.
. . .

He stops. He cannot think the next thought. It cannot be thought by him. We sit in silence. There. Some of it's been said. Words have been formed and have left him. They have passed through the air. He lifts his cup and stares at the coffee grounds. Silence. A thickening.

As the ship moves to its berth its engines begin to increase their speed while, at the same time, its propellers are reversed in order to slow the vessel down. Large washes of water emerge from the bow. The ship vibrates and shudders, rattling not only the coffee cups and plates but the table as well, sending ripples through the hull in what sounds like a small death rattle, tons of metal protesting at the change of direction. Then the ship begins to move sideways. The *Stena Britannica* has tunnel thrusters at its bow, a set of propellers set into the front keel. It pulls itself sideways towards the dockside. With tremendous delicacy, a giant on tiptoes, it moves towards its berthing point. We watch the docking ropes being lifted onto the quayside.

There were no signs in Holland.
What do you mean no signs?
No signs saying 'Keine Juden'. No Jews.
Oh yes.
No yellow stars on the shops when we got to Amsterdam.
. . .
No one spitting at me.

A Tannoy calls all car owners to proceed to the embarkation point on floor six. We collect our cases from the cabin and settle into the blue plastic chairs at the embarkation point. Other passengers have already arrived there. They're sitting on their cases or are slumped onto chairs, yawning, sleep still present in their bodies. The lorry drivers have assembled nearby, fidgeting, feet tapping. A further announcement is made calling all truckers to their lorries and then a chain is lifted and we, the car owners, proceed down to the car deck. Today the lift has broken, which means that we will all have to walk down twelve flights of stairs to the car deck. I offer to carry my father's suitcase for him but he declines and walks down the steps himself. He is still strong enough to catch the people up in front of us, his energy far out of step with his age. We arrive at the car deck, load our cases into my brother's car, start it and move slowly along the nearly empty belly of the ship. Its bowels echo, and we taste car fumes on our tongues as we leave through the ship's mouth, past the men in orange signalling us to drive on the correct side of the road, over the brown steel ramps, past the dock gates and into Holland.

2.10

When Mr Bubyage became ill he was taken to hospital and while there he asked my father to sort out both of his beehives. My father agreed and so I went to Mr Bubyage's house with him, brooding and wordless on the grey vinyl seats of the latest Mini. Initially I waited by the front door of Mr Bubyage's red-brick terraced house while my father went inside. But curiosity overwhelmed me and so I stepped along his own carefully laid concrete path, past his black bicycle, and ventured into the small dark rooms that were his home. It was practically bare. Coats were on the bed instead of blankets and he used candles to see by at night. It was spotless and there was nothing in it, apart from a small iron bed; not even an electric fire or a photograph. I moved carefully around the house, which smelt of carbolic soap, but saw nothing at all except two white string vests on a single wire coat hanger attached to a hook on the bedroom wall. But when I opened a small door in the kitchen, I found myself in a tiny shelved larder. Looking up, I saw a wall of amber jars of honey, perhaps a hundred, stacked and dated and glinting in the light that came in from the small, high, reinforced window in the corner of the whitewashed room.

Later that afternoon I found myself in a bright summer's

field at Mr Bubyage's hives. My father had asked his friend Mr Jones to help with the bees and when we arrived he was already there, dressed from head to foot in his beekeeping equipment, with its white netting and circular hat. Mr Jones was going to move the bees from Mr Bubyage's hive to his own. His bees had recently swarmed, leaving his hives empty. Mr Jones's hive was situated more than the necessary 3 miles from Mr Bubyage's, the distance needed to ensure that the bees did not get confused after a move. 'The rule,' said Mr Jones,

is that if bees are going to be moved from one hive to another they have to be moved either less than 3ft or more than 3 miles. Longer moves are more successful than shorter ones. Close moves are too confusing as the bees follow known markers to and from their hive. If the entrance has been moved they just don't know how to find it. And they are usually exhausted after collecting pollen. After the move the next generations know nothing else.

Having finished his speech, Mr Jones adjusted his beekeeping garb and approached the hive with care, lifting out the stacked frames one by one until he came to the queen. Despite his confidence, the bees became agitated and started to make a dark humming noise. This went on for some time until suddenly out of the hive a new virgin queen escaped into the light, ascending with startling rapidity high into the air, the male bees following her at speed in a furious, weaving dance, desperate to mate with her in order to become the progenitor of the new hive. The queen and her entourage flew so high that for several minutes they disappeared into the sky, higher than the eye could see. Then the rest of the bees – the workers – began, with a most disconcerting and threatening noise, to leave the hive in huge numbers, tipping out of the small entrances in seemingly endless and improbable streams and flying agitatedly until there were so many that they darkened the sunlight in the field. Their vigorous activity in the air crescendoed quickly and alarmingly, their collective noise warning everything away, clearly confusing the surrounding birds who called to each other and flew higher, keeping a wide berth. Mr Jones urged us to remain still for some time until the bees began to collect nearby on a tree stump covered with ivy. It took a long time for the bees to settle, to cluster together and to cover each other in a dense mass. Mr Jones explained that they had found where the new queen had landed and so had gone there to protect her. He also told us that bees don't kill by stinging but by suffocating their victim. They crawl into a human's nose, down their throat and into their lungs. And so we must keep our distance from the tree stump.

Nevertheless, with my breath held, my father and I walked towards the swarm and, together, stood close to it for several minutes. And it was there that I was able to observe closely the intense, dark, writhing, fearsome power of a swarm.

3.1

Although the approach to the Hook of Holland on the *Stena Britannica* was sunny and bright, a coastal fog has risen up from the land. We drive immediately into it. It is so dense it's as though we're underwater, the light diffused, objects blurred. It's a surprise after the brightness out at sea, but this happens occasionally along the coast at this time of year, when a hot sun heats a cold autumn sea. I open the car window, put my hand into the air, feel the back of it cool as it traces a line through the soporific ether. We move at a dawdle, letting the fog fill the car until it's freezing. 'Reminds me of Welsh weather,' says my father.

Partly because it's difficult to see any signs and partly due to my general ineptitude when it comes to directions, I realise I don't know where we are. It's not just the fog, it's the Dutch road signs that have confused me, the road we're on changing its number as we drive along it.

Where-the-bloody-hell-are-we?
I'm not sure.
Don't tell me you don't know?
Could be on the N211 or the E30. Or the A4.
It can only be one of them.

It seems to be all three.

How-can-it-be-all-three?

I don't know.

Didn't you bring a map?

I brought a map.

So where is it?

The one I brought with me doesn't have this area of the Netherlands on it.

What are you talking about?

The map I've got only has half of Holland on it.

You bought a map of half of Holland?

I bought a map of Germany that also has the eastern half of Holland on it. Unfortunately we're still in the western half. I brought some directions that I've written down.

So why can't you use them?

I've looked at them and they don't make much sense.

It's the fog.

I stop the car at the side of the road and get out, partly to see if I can work out where we are, partly to try to get a grip of myself.

There are no people about and there is no traffic. The world is at peace as I stand resting my arm on the car's roof, the blanket of water droplets minimising the passage of sound, the dull, metallic noises of the ship now absent, the fog's soft air kind to my lungs and skin. The houses nearby have large sharply angled roofs laid with red Spanish tiles. They have wide eaves that cast faint shadows around the upper part of their walls. Other houses have been constructed in the shape of traditional Dutch barns. All are brick-built, many of them painted white, grey, black, dark brown. All have small gardens in front of them, ankle-height hedges, strips of grass, flower beds of dark soil, low-trimmed trees. One house has four pear trees trained to grow along a set of wires tied to one of its walls. The branches are dark and without leaves and so look like an ink drawing on white paper. The houses further back are only hinted at – a glint of windows, a mysterious flicker of lights, soft halos, pearlescent air. I get back in the car. We pass along Molenweg, Haagweg, Molenslag and onto Schelpenpad. As we travel the roads become narrower and then, worryingly, sandy. The road finishes. It comes to an end. I stop the car, step onto a thin layer of sand, the kind of sand that is blown off a beach. In front of us a dyke slopes 30ft in the air with steps leading to its top.

I walk up these concrete steps to the top of the dyke to see the sea we have recently been floating on rolling with thick mist. In the distance I hear the low bleats of a foghorn. Below me small waves smooth a flat beach. I walk down the dyke, step onto hard, wet sand. Large amounts of spindrift have collected on the shore. Yellow and white froth. My father stands behind me.

How can you have not brought a map?

We return to the car. I retrace my route as best I can. Patches of fog lift a few feet off the ground. It is as though a theatre curtain has been partially lifted at the play's opening, revealing the feet and ankles of the characters and the lowest parts of the stage scenery. In Essex this fog is known as 'fret' and it is certainly causing me to fret. It's an odd portent to the beginning of the journey.

> A pathetic fallacy.
> *What is?*
> The fog at the beginning of a journey. Symbolising our confusion.
> *If you say so.*
> Ruskin.

We drive along the tops of dykes on single-lane roads, their considerable height above the surrounding land a surprise.

> *Why can't you use your phone?*
> I forgot to tell the phone company I'm coming abroad.
> It's not working.
> *How you survive in life I just don't know.*

Below us the edges of the fields are visible through the white air. They are planted with winter cabbages and Brussels sprouts. Long rows are set upon the black soil that has been reclaimed from the sea.

We leave the dykes, pass through acres of sprawling

greenhouses. Many of their roof lights are open, breaking up the repeated pattern of their ridged roofs. The rhythm of these extended glass structures echoes the repeated chords of minimalist music, a Philip Glass concerto of greenhouse roofs. At times they are present on both sides of the road so that it seems for a while that we are driving through a glass-covered countryside, the dense foliage of the plants growing inside them living in a parallel, windless world of warmth and humidity.

Eventually the mist lifts. Now I can see the road and so stop at a garage to buy a map. Unfortunately there are no maps of the Netherlands for sale in this garage and so I ask the man serving me if he could tell me where we are. He takes out an old worn book of maps from behind the counter and looks at it carefully. He scrutinises the pages, flicking them over one way, then back again until, without enthusiasm, he points his finger at a page and states, 'We are here.' I look carefully at where he's pointing but can't make sense of our position. He lifts up the book of maps and I realise from the way he's gripping the cover that he's been holding the maps upside down. He's been pretending to be able to map-read. The journey is already a bizarre enough event without being directed by a man who can't read maps and who holds them upside down. Luckily the woman who is also serving petrol helps. She takes the maps, turns them and shows us where we are and how to get onto the road that will take us towards Germany.

We pass through the neat roads of The Hague, under

bridges with embankments covered in trailing ivies, past the backs of houses and flats, their walls laid in symmetrical patterns of yellow and red brick, past small parks and tiny streets and individual shops that haven't yet opened. We drive through a series of underpasses, their dark interiors flecked intermittently with light shining through gaps in their roofs, skylights set into the streets above. We pass large buildings coated in glass, a few people cycling on upright bikes, a couple of dog walkers, the occasional jogger, until we move away from the city centre towards the suburbs and then further – first past occasional fields and then into the countryside.

We enter the Dutch motorway system that sweeps harmoniously through the Netherlands. These motorways are quiet due to the particular compound that is used for their surfacing. Their signage is clear and thoughtfully positioned, the curves of the road set at particular radii, which is calming, encouraging reflective thought as we drive. The countryside stretches into the distance from all directions, a minimal, unimposing landscape that shows off its sky, its cerulean air.

We stop at a service station, the AVIA Oldenzaal. I fill the car with diesel. We enter its adjoining café. We sit at a small square table covered in a red-and-white checked tablecloth. The woman who serves us is tall and kindly and smiles gently at my father. She is dressed in a uniform with a headscarf made from the same material as the tablecloths. We choose coffee and Dutch apple pie. I savour the bitterness of the thick black coffee, the zest of the pie and its light pastry. 'Particularly delicious,' says my father, as he devours it at speed. 'Cinnamon and nutmeg,' he tells me, before finishing it and resting his fork on the plate.

We'll be in Germany soon.

3.2

There were two ways to drive up Pentrosfa by car. The first and normal way was to slow down in Wellington Road, turn the right angle into Pentrosfa, slow to a stop, change carefully into first gear and then climb the hill gently, circumnavigating its potholes by weaving tentatively across the road from one side to the other at little more than walking speed. Everyone drove up Pentrosfa like this except for my father. His chosen technique was the second way and he was the only one who attempted it. His way involved speeding up just before the corner, pumping the brakes with a rapid motion of his feet and legs, slamming down the gears while at the same time in a flurry of elbows and hands rapidly spinning the Mini's large, two-pronged steering wheel sharply to one side. The effect of all of this was to fling the car around the corner, its tyres squealing onto the bottom of the hill that he then attacked. While everyone else meandered around the road looking for the smoothest part, my father set the car in a straight line, put his foot flat on the accelerator and, ignoring the holes and rocks, encouraged the red Mini to hit them straight on, which meant that at times it lifted off the ground, rather as a stone does when it is skimmed across the water. The effect of this was to send the car's engine screaming, for an engine without a wheel on the ground revs furiously and painfully, and so as the Mini lurched and jumped from one cavity to another it emitted a high-pitched wail.

The sound of hurt metal coupled with the sight of my father's body bouncing around inside the car, his head hitting against its roof, created a sense of awe among my friends and incredulity among their parents. As we could hear the noise of his Mini before we could see it if we were playing in the road, we would rush to the safety of its edges to watch the spectacle of his car as it came up the hill towards us. Skidding to a halt in a cloud of dust, always in exactly the same place, he would then emerge from the car quickly, slam the door and stroll purposefully through the front gate, up Mr Bubyage's path, through the black-and-cream front door into the house, his body powerful, his hair tousled, his brown shoes polished.

This was the time when Paddy Hopkirk was winning rallies in Minis, their small size and improbable ability to hold the road around corners allowing them to beat far more powerful cars in the Welsh hills, and even winning the Monte Carlo rally three times.

However, there was a fundamental difference between my father's Mini and a Mini rally car. Mini rally cars were heavily strengthened with metal bars on the insides of the doors and had roll cages, sump-guards and other structural reinforcements. As my father's Mini was standard, and therefore without reinforcements, he periodically wrecked it, either by hitting the sump so that the oil drained out of the engine or once by banging the car so hard that the front wheel fell off.

He was always crashing. After one of his most serious crashes, into a tractor in Llanelwedd, which he was lucky to survive, he took the whole family down in the new green Mini to look at the skid marks he had left while destroying the old red one. After parking on the verge he got out of the car and walked into the middle of the road where he began, at some risk to himself, to pace the long black skid marks, a pair of tortured liquorice lines that stretched out before him. The whole family sat in the Mini watching him through its tiny windscreen as, with measured strides, he walked carefully along the middle of the road, following the strange snaking lines. After completing the calculation he walked back towards us and swung the driver's door open, proclaiming with a tremendous sense of satisfaction as he settled onto the red fabric of the seat,

They're 33 yards long! I must have been doing at least 70.

And with that we set off, passing along the twisting road that follows the River Wye from Llanelwedd to Llanfaredd and then on to Aberedw, crossing small, metal, riveted bridges and those made of stone. The Wye is wide at this point and therefore shallow and so chirrups as it passes over its bed of stones, conversing, as it so often does in summer, lightly with the dense foliage that bends over its water.

The effect of my father's crashes was left on me. The day I was given a pedal car for my birthday I immediately started driving it down Pentrosfa and crashing it into our gatepost.

As this was an old pedal car the metal was thick and wouldn't dent. In the end I had to go to the top of the hill and at what then seemed to me like terrific speed slam it again into the gatepost. The force was such that I was thrown against the steering wheel. It hurt so much that I cried, but I was proud that I had dented it. Bizarrely, my father couldn't make the connection and was unable to understand this destructive behaviour, even becoming cross and hurt about it, wanting to know why I was trying to destroy my new present. But the logic had entered my composition. Cars were there to be driven fast. And destroyed.

3.3

As we approach the Holland–Germany border near the town of Luttermolen, the railway track between Berlin and Amsterdam crosses the road above us. It's suspended on a bridge constructed with cylindrical concrete pillars and as we move towards it a white high-speed ICE train appears, moving at great speed, the long sloping nose of its engine pushing away volumes of air, its carriages for some time present on the bridge in a smooth and fluid motion, curving confidently before descending down to ground level where the tracks run for a short distance beside the Autobahn. The train is moving faster than our car and disappears into the distance as we pass under the bridge it's just crossed. A few minutes later we pass under another bridge of pale-green scaffolding covered in CCTV cameras, the border between Holland and Germany.

Germany?
Yes.

In Germany the Autobahn is narrower. It has tighter bends than either the Dutch or British motorways. It was constructed during the 1930s, much earlier than any other similar roads in other countries. Building took place under the leadership of Fritz Todt, inspector general for German Roadways, who in 1940 went on to become the minister of armaments and munitions. The road is bumpier and noisier and is made of concrete with compression joints. We pass signs to the town of Bad Bentheim.

Bentheim is where the Nazis got off my train.
Really?
Bentheim's the last German station before Holland.
Shall we stop?
If you want to.

We take the exit to Bad Bentheim and drive immediately into thick woods. The light on the road dances in front of us. We drive for 3 or 4 miles, pass under a railway bridge, turn right into the station car park and get out at Bad Bentheim's station. We walk across the car park onto the train platform. The station building is made of brick. Some of the bricks have been laid in a pattern and have dark brown wood attached to them.

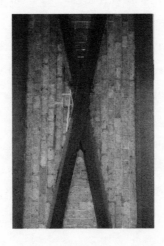

This is where we stopped. I remember it.

We walk to the end of the platform. Disused railway lines covered in brambles recede into the woods. Silver birch crowd the sidings. Their branches face up towards the sky. A couple of shunters whose fronts are painted in thick yellow–and–black lines in the shape of an inverted 'V' are parked. One track stretches into the distance. My father grips his stomach.

I need the lavatory. Quickly.
There's one just outside in the car park. I noticed it when we came in.

We walk quickly back to the public toilets. My father disappears into one of them. I turn and walk back onto the platform. I lie on the ground with my face down. I feel the cold of the platform push itself into my body and into my face. I lay my cheek onto its gritty surface. I feel that there is a weight upon my back. It presses me into the ground. I can't stand up. I am bolted down again. The ground calls me. I kiss it and then push my hands against the platform and get back up. My father emerges from the toilets and walks towards me. He is small and bent.

I was towards the front of the train.
Here?
We were all thirsty.
Was it hot?

Very hot. The train took hours. Trains shook in those days.

What was the date?

The last Saturday of July 1939.

As he speaks my father's body contracts, his eyes withdraw, his shoulders hunch. He shivers. He becomes a different colour. He bites his nails.

This is the last place I saw Nazis in uniform.

. . .

They had dogs.

. . .

I need to sit down.

I point to the station hotel on the other side of the platform, the Bentheimer Hof. We walk under the railway bridge towards it, slowly, my father shaking as lorries pass us, loaded with logs extracted from the surrounding forests. We enter the hotel and stand in front of a dark wooden reception desk. We ring a bell. No one comes. We walk through the deserted building into a large dining room set with napkins and glasses. Its walls are dark ochre, its ceiling a clotted cream. Heavy maroon embroidered curtains hang from each of the windows. One of the internal walls is made from oak and has stained glass in it. Glints of ruby and blackcurrant fleck the air.

We sit down at one of the tables and my father is overcome with tiredness, his legs suddenly frail. He sits heavily onto a chair. A tall woman arrives, seemingly from nowhere. She wears silver wire-framed glasses and has orthodontically cor-rected teeth. My father asks for '*ein Kaffee schwarz*'. We drink in silence. His hands are quivering. His bitten nails have flecks of blood on them.

3.4

Paul was my friend. He lived opposite us on the other side of Pentrosfa. His father's name was Bryn and, as everyone knew, during the war Bryn had flown in Lancaster bombers or, as he called them, Avro Lancasters. Bryn, Paul told me confidentially, had been the man who looked after all four of the engines when the plane was in the sky, and he used to live 'in an air base'. Bryn was petite and distinguished. He was so socially able and so charmingly adept that he seemed to have emerged fully formed from the brown-and-cream Bakelite television in the corner of his primrose sitting room, with its bay window and its picture rail. There was something in the air surrounding him that was so assured and emanated such confidence that he seemed to belong to another world. His voice was resonant and unapologetic. Each of his sentences, to their end, were unwaveringly confident in their significance. He wore white flannel trousers with cream shirts and brown polished leather shoes, and an array of cardigans, beige or cornflower or mauve, patterned in diamond shapes, some with hints of fandango pink, each with bone buttons. His hair was blond and thickly curled and he wore horn–rimmed glasses. He was truly debonair. And although he never mentioned it, the whole village knew that he had sat on one of *those* brown leather seats in one of *those* cockpits staring out through *that* thick glass while his bomber discharged its munitions over Berlin, reducing its streets to rubble, its shameful history erased bomb by bomb by him and his fellows as they terrorised and killed the guilty and the innocent alike.

And yet here they were together, my father and Bryn, standing on Mr Bubyage's path, making small talk, the soothing murmur of their voices carrying across the evening air while sparrows spruced themselves in the dry dust of Pentrosfa and the occasional blue tit picked at the foiled tops of milk bottles that had been left on doorsteps from the morning delivery. Together they stood, strong and powerful, in the pomp of their lives, their shadows lengthening beside them as their fluid voices flowed through their bodies, their legs planted firmly on the ground, their hips level, their shoulders back, their cheerful laughs rippling up through their ribcages and out through the creases of their eyes, and it made no sense that one had participated in the destruction of the city the other had escaped from, the unspeakable cord that joined them.

It was Paul who showed me the secret one evening – the dog whips on the wall of the garden shed. Short, leather whips, five of them nailed to the wall in a row. And it was he who told me that his father asked him to choose which one he should be whipped with if he had done the slightest thing wrong and was to be punished. And so I finally understood the occasional strangled noises I heard at night through the thin glass of my bedroom window. They were from Paul being whipped in the shed in his garden – short, contained sobs, in the cold, as the frost composed of my sister's and my solidifying breath began to settle on the window's glass.

Bryn's front room was covered in photographs of him with his crew in front of his bomber in what can only be described as decorative poses. There were no signs of fear or unreason in his front room. His Avro Lancaster bomber was noble and heroic, as were his crew, their smiling, laconic faces glistening in the picture frames, staring out at us as we drank glasses of lemon barley water and ate slices of white bread. In that room there was no record of the smell of adrenaline or the viciously cold air at 16,000ft or the fact that over half the men who flew in Avro Lancasters had died, most falling through the air before they did so, trapped inside what were about to become their riveted shrouds, their brains racing as they plummeted, the sound of the bombers' engines filling their heads, aware as they tried unsuccessfully to scrabble out of their descending infernos, just before their incineration, of the design decision that had made the escape hatches in Avro Lancasters too small for most men to get through when a parachute was attached to their backs.

It was Paul whom I had fought with fists in my garden on Mr Bubyage's path, surrounded by the older children who had come up to our house to arrange the fight and to cheer Paul on. I was puzzled by this. Until then he and I had been the best of friends but somehow he had suddenly grown to hate me, as my friends suddenly had too. 'Why do you want to fight?' I asked him. 'You're a Jew,' he replied, 'that's why.'

I remember him taking off his shirt, surrounded by the red-brick wall topped with semicircular bricks, like the shape of lemon slices, and me taking off my glasses and hitting him and the strange feeling of my fist against his flesh, then being hit by him and the strange lack of pain it gave me, more a sort of warmth, and us both bleeding, and the fight going on and on, and the pain not bothering me. Even then I could tell that this was odd: I didn't mind the bruises because the bruises put me back into my body, away from my mind with its cascade of fear and unrest. Bruises were a momentary rest and so never feared. And even welcomed.

3.5

As we leave the Bentheimer Hof we notice a path opposite us that leads directly into the woods. We decide to walk along it, light waving at us, leaves falling, the path's stones under our feet, the occasional sounds of birds breaking the air, the thickening trees creating a gloom. Inside the woods we come across a large sandstone needle named 'The Pyramide'. It is about 40ft high. It has carved on one of its sides: C. F. B. S. LANDKRIESS. GRAFSCHAFT. BENTHEIM. On another side there's a stone relief of a man clubbing a dragon to death. His powerful body twists from his ankles to his neck, his shoulders pivot away from his hips, his eye is on the exact spot where he is about to strike the dragon, his large, metal-tipped club held high, as a baseball player might look as he or she is about to hit the ball. The dragon is cowering, wounded and damaged, next to the entrance to a castle. On the third face are the words ERECTA PERENNAT with a stone relief of five men lifting the Pyramide into position. According to the sign next to it, it was erected in 1710 and is part of a sequence of stone monuments located in this forest.

We carry on walking until we reach the end of the path, which opens into a small manicured park with sculptures and fountains in it. A few people dressed in white clothes wander about, some on their own, some smoking, some on their phones, some sitting on benches staring into the middle distance. An anorexic teenager walks between her parents, her hips stiff, her feet flat, her parents' grief radiating from their bodies, at odds with their brave smiling faces that turn towards their daughter.

In the distance we hear the sound of murmuring. We move towards it. We come upon a wire-mesh fence behind which is an open, heated swimming pool. Fifty or sixty people are exercising in its blue chlorinated water. They are stretching and jumping. They are throwing balls to each other. Some sit in floating rings, some are on the edges of the pool. Some are wrapped in layers of towels, all are laughing and chattering, steam rising off the pool's warm water, condensing in the cold air above, their voices light, like the sounds of birds. 'It's a spa,' says my father. 'Bad Bentheim means it's a spa town; this park must be part of it.'

We carry on towards a small white building and see people drinking tall glasses of lager through one of its windows. Others are eating sandwiches and cakes. We circle back around the house then back through the woods along the bark-chipped path, past the Pyramide again. We walk back into Bad Bentheim, through its park and to its medieval castle.

We sit together on one of its castellated walls high above the surrounding ground, the view of the countryside below us.

> *The German railways charged single fares for each Jewish man and woman transported to each concentration camp. Under-twelves half price. Children under four free. The Nazi guards were charged return fares.*

We return to the car and rejoin the E30 towards Hannover. My father is constantly gripped by a pain in his stomach. We stop frequently. We pull into lay-bys that have public toilets in them, waiting our turn with other road users. At one point he goes into the toilet, returns to the car, sits in its front seat and then immediately gets out of the car and rejoins the queue to go back into the toilet. 'I've always had a tricky stomach,' he says on his return. It's true that my childhood was interrupted by his sudden shouts of 'Out of the way, I've got the squits!' as he marched to the nearest toilet, though he never, ever called it 'a toilet'. 'A toilet is something you do, not go to,' he would say, insisting instead on calling it 'the lavatory'.

He returns to the car.

Two sisters from the Baader–Meinhof Gang were from Bad Bentheim.

Really?

I remember reading about it ages ago. One of them murdered that industrialist.

Did they?

They kidnapped him and then they executed him. His body was found in the boot of a car.

3.6

After snow fell it would drift, blown by the wind, to the lower parts of fields, sometimes reaching our waists. We would wade into it until we were up to our chests and couldn't move, our limbs pinned by its unlikely weight, laughing, standing next to each other, watching the cold white powder flutter then settle upon us. At the tops of fields snow was thinner. It was there that we would run, chasing each other and our dogs, throwing snowballs and taking wooden sledges and capsizing down the hill, soaked by the snow that stuck to our clothes in small, hard silver balls of ice. To celebrate its arrival we would stay out for most of the day in woollen coats with gloves and hats. Once I stayed out for too long. I let cold creep into my bones, turn their marrow raw, and into my chest cavity too. Cold took up residence inside me. Afterwards it became impossible to chase it out and get warm again. It was later that evening that my breathing worsened, tightening my chest and sending me quietly to stand by the kitchen stove, my back pressed against its reassuring solidity, the intercostal muscles between each of my ribs comforted by its radiating heat.

At that time the slight constriction in my chest seemed of little importance, my back bore up well, my body was only slightly bent and although the air that passed through it prickled my chest, it was manageable and not at all terrifying. Even later that evening, when I was lying in the ice-cold air of my bedroom, pressed down by the weight of the blankets and eiderdowns lying upon me and with two towels wrapped tightly around me, one around my chest and the other around my head, it hardly seemed more serious. Because of this I got up the next morning and attended school. There too, among the dusty hymn books, the hessian-covered arithmetic books and the yellowing pages of the grammar books whose words danced inchoately in front of me, my chest held up, a minor tickle dancing in my lungs, but no more. It was as though any admission of my impending illness would immediately flood my chest with the sticky, yellow fluid that would later fill my lungs, arriving as it did in waves, the infection weighting me, a sack of stones drowning me, fighting, it seemed, to remove me from this world and take me, a tiny step at a time, to my grave.

As it was I stood, when I could, with my legs pressed against the cast iron of the school radiators until my skin became red, looking down at my feet in their woollen socks pulled up tight over my knees and holding my green striped V-necked jumper close to me. To deal with the situation I learned to hold my breath for as long as I could and then breathe out slowly, for it was the breathing out that had become difficult. Exhalation became an act of concerted will while, oddly, inhalation remained easy, the available air clear and cold as it passed into my lungs, and although it tickled the respiratory bronchioles and alveoli in my lungs it did not as yet throw them into spasms. Later I would find out that the thinnest part of a lung, at only one-fifth of a millionth of a metre in thickness, a width oxygen molecules can move through so allowing them into the bloodstream, cannot be seen by a microscope and must be measured electromagnetically. It is through this membrane that waste carbon dioxide crosses the other way, from blood to air. The whole of mammalian life is maintained by the thinnest membrane, a skin stretched and stretched until it is one-cell thick.

The expulsion of my lungs' air required me to sustain huge amounts of concentration, pushing it out through the infection that had gripped and coated their membranes. I had to sustain a continual focus on my ribcage's shape and position to try to reduce the whistling as it passed through the narrowing constrictions. Because of this I learned to move my ribs as little as possible, developing a method where I made myself breathe from the very top of my lungs, panting deliberately in tiny, shallow breaths, just like a dog trying to overcome too much heat. This helped me avoid the lakes of fluid that were forming inside them.

When I eventually started coughing I could not stop. My father remained unimpressed, saying, 'For goodness sake cough it up and spit it out.' I would do as I was told, spitting small balls of greenish sputum, some striated with blood, onto the grass, or the road, or into the kitchen sink. 'That's good, that's better,' my father would go on encouragingly. 'Give it a hard belt.' Eventually my mother shouted at him, insisting that he listen to my chest with his stethoscope. After placing the cold metal disc carefully over the front and back of my chest he proclaimed, 'Yes, he does have a tickle.' And so later that afternoon I was taken to the small cottage hospital where my father worked.

After entering the red-brick building we walked down its long corridors until we found ourselves in front of a sign that ordered, in red capital letters: KEEP OUT: DANGER: RADIA-TION, DANGER OF DEATH. The size of the sign as well as the threatening font brought me up sharp. 'Wait here,' said my father. 'I'll go and get Mr Williams. He's the radiographer and he'll unlock the door.' I stood by the white metal door, my head reaching slightly above its long brass handle, noticing its protruding hinges, its three chipped padlocks. Nurses in blue uniforms padded past me, pushing trolleys with large black rubber wheels, each carrying an array of medical equip-ment, dressings, kidney bowls, scalpels, oxygen tanks. They travelled seamlessly along the corridor whose floor was laid with hundreds of small square tiles in shades of cream and mint flecked with azure in patterns not unlike the feathers of a peacock.

Mr Williams arrived carrying a large ring of keys. He was a powerfully built, silent man with thick black hair. His high forehead had a set of white scars on it, as though a young child had squiggled them onto his skull with a thin-nibbed pen, and he wore large, thick, black-framed glasses with dark tinted lenses through which I could see the whites of his eyes, which seemed particularly bright, a ring of white around his irises.

He undid the locks to the door carefully. His black leather

shoes, like my father's, were highly polished in the manner of an ex-military man, the toes shining brightly, gleaming, his fingernails were filed, their crescents a vivid white, their tips evenly curved. Eventually he pushed open the door and asked me quietly to strip off my clothes down to my underpants, which I did, folding them carefully and placing them on the metal and canvas chair situated in the corner of the room. He then pointed to the machine in the centre of the room, which I stepped onto and which had a large metal plate in front of it. Another plate, fixed to a small gate, was swung in behind me so that I became sandwiched between them. After positioning both gates carefully, Mr Williams and my father both left me and, to my concern, moved into a small cubicle situated in the large room I was standing in. 'We have come into the cubicle in the corner just in case,' Mr Williams told me. 'Just in case of what?' I replied. 'Just in case we're affected over time by the ferocity of the X-rays. They're accumulative, you see.' I nodded, not really understanding what accumulative was but feeling more isolated and anxious than I usually did. 'When I press this switch, the X-rays will go through your body,' said Mr Williams, leaning his body out of the cubicle, his tinted lenses suddenly looking curiously enigmatic. '*Through* my body?' I said. 'That's right.' '*All the way* through?' I said. 'All the way through, except for when they catch on your bones,' replied Mr Williams, his eyes now averted, his hands with their filed nails hanging beside him. 'They catch on my bones?' I said. 'Your bones and any infection you might have if it's very serious,' he went on. 'Very serious?' The tone of his words had cast shadows of doubt inside me. 'You must remain still when I press the switch,' he said, raising his voice to ensure I could hear him clearly. 'It says danger of death on the door,' I said, in as loud a voice as I could. 'Only if you have too many of them,' Mr Williams replied, his eyes still averted to the floor. 'Where are they? The X-rays?' I went on. 'It's all very complicated,' replied Mr Williams, 'so just stand still.' I imagined the X-rays waiting excitedly for the moment they could whistle through my body and then out through the walls and windows, screeching to each other in their gleeful new-found freedom, delighting in their sobriquet of 'X' rather than a retiring and sensible 'P' or a strong, steadfast 'A'. 'But does that mean it's a bit dangerous?' I asked. 'Yes, I have to be very careful,' went on Mr Williams, aware perhaps that his future was known to him and that his fate was being decided incrementally as he spoke to me.

The room I was standing in smelt of soap from years of constant disinfection, and had been converted inside the original Victorian hospital. The lower third of its walls was laid with white square porcelain tiles that had dark-green grout between them. The upper two thirds of the walls showed the original exposed bricks that had been overpainted in white, some of it peeling away in patches around the high windows with their vertical iron bars. The room possessed a thick aura of anxiety. It was like walking into a soup of green air caused by the procession of people who had come here over the years, agitated, more or less naked, waiting to hear their sentence, knowing that something was wrong with them but not sure quite what. 'Don't cough as we take the X-ray,' said Mr Williams, but his instruction brought, as it inevitably would, a cough from me at the exact moment he released the switch that made the plates in the X-ray machine emit a low buzz. Because I had coughed and heaved droplets across the room at the wrong moment, Mr Williams had to reset the machine. 'I'm going to have to do it again because you coughed. Try not to cough,' he repeated firmly as he adjusted the metal plates around me, but it was useless – my lungs splattered snot and phlegm around the room as he pressed the switch again. 'He can't keep still,' said Mr Williams to my father. 'Probably not his fault, but I don't think we should expose him to any more radiation.' 'If you say so,' said my father. 'You can't be too careful,' said Mr Williams. 'The government guidelines are far too lenient as far as I'm concerned. They allow for far too much exposure.' 'I don't think you have to worry,' said my father, and with that I was allowed to collect my clothes and dress, afterwards standing next to my father and the funereal Mr Williams in the protected cubicle, watching the X-ray of the inside of my body as it was developed in front of my eyes, the processing chemicals catching my tongue and stinging my eyes.

After the photographic film had been placed in various liquids it was dried and placed in front of a light box on the wall where it revealed the view of my ribs and lungs, a glimpse of my interior, the contours strange and ghostly. Both my father and Mr Williams suddenly became very quiet as they concentrated, before pointing at a particular part of the image of my body. 'Look,' said my father, breaking the silence cheerfully, 'there's dense patches on your lungs. That's where the X-rays got caught and couldn't go all the way through you, the same as your bones – can you see?' 'Did all the others go all the way through me?' I asked. 'That's correct,' said my father. 'Now, you'd better leave the room for a minute,' he went on. 'It's not good,' I heard Mr Williams say as I was leaving the cubicle. 'It's not too bad,' replied my father. 'It's pneumonia,' said Mr Williams. 'Even though the image is shaky because he moved, you can see the clouds on his lungs. He's seriously ill.'

Afterwards my father and I walked back along the tiled corridor in silence, the occasional rubber-wheeled trolley gliding towards us then smoothly passing by, the wheels eerily quiet, each steered by a nurse, hands placed upon the metal bar. Further down the corridor we met a senior nurse with a dark-blue-and-white hat on her head who, it turned out, was the matron. 'How is he?' she said to my father. 'He's fine,' replied my father, 'a patch on the lungs, that's all.' 'He looks blue around the gills,' said the matron, her large brown eyes kind and gentle. 'He'll be all right, he'll be fine,' said my father. 'What do you want to be when you grow up?' asked the matron suddenly. 'I don't know,' I coughed. 'A doctor like your father?' she went on. I evaded the question by retreating along the corridor, my father catching me up, his footsteps clattering slightly as his heels struck the peacock-patterned floor tiles. We walked through the dark wooden door of the hospital out into the cold air where I started to cough again. 'Look,' said my father, suddenly irritable and impatient, 'the insides of your lungs are, if you stretched them out and laid them on the floor, the same size as one side of a tennis court, so a bit of damage on some of it won't hurt you – I've seen much worse. Stop making a fuss.' Not making a fuss was particularly important to my father. It was to be avoided if at all possible. He never wanted to ask for anything and encouraged us not to either. 'Come on, let's get in the car.'

He didn't speak to me during the car ride home. It was not his fault that he was preoccupied with other things. So was I, what with scars and lungs the size of tennis courts and X-rays flying straight through me, some of which were caught in my bones and so presumably, though I didn't like to think of it, still there. If he was unavailable to me, I was to him, and although the weight of this fell onto my shoulders from an early age, and although I spent much effort in attempting to offer a corrective between our two silences, it was how it was. Even when I asked him about Mr Williams's scarred forehead he was cursory. 'Dunkirk,' he said, as though this explained everything, and so stopped any further questioning as he drove the car down the peculiar slope outside the hospital.

He remained silent during the rapid progress through town in the green Mini, stayed wordless while he swerved around the sharp, steep corner before Pentrosfa, remained quiet during the car's alarming shaking as he accelerated it up the hill to our house. He remained lost in thought, the long gear stick of the car wobbling, the strained whine of the engine hitting our ears, the metal ledge in the Mini's interior, the cold vinyl of the car seats, filling both our minds.

3.7

The Autobahn suddenly stops at a set of traffic lights on a crossroads in the town of Bad Oeynhausen. Unusually the road has changed from an Autobahn to the road of a provincial town. We pull into a JET petrol station that sits alongside a long glass building used for car washes – the *Waschstraße*. It is painted bright, frog-green and has a sign on it: *Power sauger, jetzt bei jeder autowäsche.*

I fill the car with diesel and, together, we enter the garage's shop. My father buys two frankfurters from the outlet in the corner that sells heated pastries and rolls. The food is lit by orange-tinted LED lights that cast a 1970s nightclub glow over the ham and sliced-cheese rolls. My father makes his order in German, the sound of his voice still unfamiliar to me as he speaks his first language. The woman serving him asks him if he's English. 'Do you think I'm English?' he replies, thrilled at the question. 'Yes,' she says, as she hands him two enormous tan-coloured frankfurters that poke out of both ends of luminous white cotton-wool bread rolls. Delighted at being thought English he holds the frankfurters up high in the air and swiftly carries them across the shop and, with some difficulty as both hands are full of frankfurters, through its spring-loaded door onto the garage forecourt. There he starts to eat the frankfurter in his right hand while standing between the petrol pumps and the carwash. He's covered both frankfurters in volumes of yellow mustard and eats the first one quietly, a smile of contentment spreading across his face, while keeping the second one in his left hand. I can see the taste takes him back in time. 'I got you one too,' he announces, his mouth full, while holding out the left-hand frankfurter and pointing it towards me, its bleached white roll catching the sun, the frankfurter itself looking as though it has come off a cheap sunbed with a faulty timer.

No thanks.
Why not?
Because I'm a vegetarian.
Are you?
Yes, I am.
You never used to be.
I know I never used to be.
Very fashionable. Being a vegetarian.
I've been one for ten years.
Have you?

My father chomps through the sausage and then wipes the corner of his mouth with a paper napkin.

Vegetarians are a touch sanctimonious, if you ask me. Mind you, you've always had that about you for some reason.

He dips his head again towards the second frankfurter and devours it even more quickly than the first, much like a dog eats, furiously, gobbling, the food barely touching the sides of his throat as it passes into his stomach. He licks his fingers.

I need a coffee.
I'll go in and get some.
Black.

I collect two coffees. Together we stand on the forecourt sipping from waxed paper cups. They have thin white plastic lids with a raised section that has three tiny holes in it through which we drink. 'Just like a mother's nipple,' says my father. 'Makes us drink like we're bloody newborn infants.' And then for some inexplicable reason I feel a contentment collect over us. A balm begins to cover the JET forecourt on Kanalstraße in Bad Oeynhausen. The stationary traffic is thick as it waits at the lights at the crossroads opposite us. In front of us there is another queue of cars waiting for the *Waschstraße* and another still for the garage. Their polluting emissions are so thick they're visible. The air tastes of fumes. They tint the sunlight grey. There is no view, no vegetation, no fresh air and no buildings of any architectural merit whatsoever, yet contentment permeates us both as we stand near the petrol pumps, where the cars' owners' bodies are contorted as they fix their eyes on the pumps' spinning numbers.

'Germans like to keep their cars clean,' my father notes happily as we watch men and women, dressed in frog-green uniforms, through the glass walls of the *Waschstraße*. They spray each car with liquid soap, hose it with high-powered water jets and dry it with chamois leathers, before hoovering and dusting the interior. Cars enter one end of the *Waschstraße* dirty and emerge fifteen minutes later gleaming. Their paint-work shines, their tyres shine, their windscreens shine, and so too it seems do their owners' faces. It is as though they have been baptised in the *Waschstraße*, the cars and their drivers renewed as they drive off back into the world again, each with a green piece of cardboard in the shape of a fir tree, the symbol of pagan life, impregnated with a powerful deodor-ant, a *Wunder-baum*, hanging and swinging from each interior driving mirror.

My father speaks.

> *Just to clarify.*
> What?
> *Your grandfather committed suicide.*
> I know.
> *So did mine.*

I pause.

> Your grandfather?
> *Yes.*
> My great-grandfather?
> *Yes. Siegfried. Your grandmother's father.*
> Suicide comes down both sides of your family?

You could say that.
What happened?
He hanged himself.

My father's lips have closed. His cheeks are raised and his eyes have narrowed.

Let's get in the car.

We walk back to my brother's car. I hold the steering wheel with both hands. I grip it tightly, engage the gears and move out into the traffic.

And this time don't get us bloody lost.

3.8

My mother's face as she heard the news about my illness at the door revealed her fury. She gave me a hot cup of tea and sent me to bed where I lay in a sweat, hardly present to the world, concentrating on every outbreath. Later my father woke me to tell me to go back to school, assuming this would aid my recovery. It was impossible for him to think that passivity and rest should be preferred to activity, for he believed that the body should, under the wish of the mind, simply obey its orders. In his eyes, movement was good while inertia was weak and indulgent and a sign of a lapsed and decadent will. 'Willpower drives you through,' he would tell me, as though pneumonia was a weakness and even possibly the first sign of self-indulgence or, even worse, bohemian tendencies, a fate that he feared and hoped his children would avoid at all costs. Somehow his exhortations for me to work despite my pneumonia revealed his understanding that I would soon drift away from his idea of how to be in the world and so then later far from him. Perhaps even then he could see that I was floating away, until I had gone from all people, then further, until I was far away even from myself, into the darker depths, hearing the voices of my grandfather and my great-grandfather, one at each ear calling to me.

I lay in bed for weeks. Each night I would be terrified that I would not survive until the morning. I just could not get the air out through the constricted bronchioles inside me. I would struggle to remain awake late into the night, listening to the sounds of the velvet air of winter, hearing my chest creaking, frightened to sleep. 'He needs to go into hospital,' I heard my mother tell my father some evenings. Then my father would listen to my chest with his stethoscope and tell me, 'It's not too bad.'

Then I would lie in bed all day, hovering in a kind of suspension, listening to the muffled sounds of the day passing through the window, the milkman in his van, the delivery of groceries, the Evans boy kick-starting his motorbike, the other children off to school. Once I watched the delivery of coal. I could see from my window men covered in soot, lifting hundredweight sacks onto their shoulders from a flatbed lorry and walking to the back door of our house before pouring the coal into our coal cellar and taking the empty hessian sacks back to the lorry where they were folded up and tied to the front of the flatbed so that they wouldn't blow away. My father counted the twenty or so sacks that he had paid for, knowing full well the phrase 'Two for you, one for the lorry'. Later, when I came downstairs wrapped in blankets, I went down to the cellar to see the coal gleaming in the dark, the small slice of compressed ancient forests broken into pieces and now in our house, each black rock surprisingly light and cold to the touch and, improbably, full of potential heat.

It took time to get better. I filled white enamel trays with phlegm covered in blood. When I returned for another X-ray with Mr Williams it showed that I had permanent scarring on my lungs. My father cheerfully told me: 'Look, it's only a bit of scarring, could be much worse. You're lucky.'

Some years later the same thing happened to Simon. He too had been out in the snow for too long one winter and caught pneumonia, and he too went to the X-ray machine with Mr Williams. But my brother was far more poorly than I ever became and so stayed in hospital next to an oxygen cylinder delivered to his bedside on one of the rubber-wheeled trolleys. Occasionally I was taken to visit him. His skin was translucent, his eczema covering his body, his sinews jutting out where his neck met his chest and shoulders, the hospital pillows framing his dark hair with white cotton. He would be either asleep or scratching, drowsy, familiar drops of blood on the inside of his elbows, skin on his fingers cracked and split, his huge dark-brown eyes ringed by black circles, the longest eyelashes, nails white and flecked with white streaks of calcium, a book about kit aeroplanes beside his bed. And my mother next to him, sitting on the hospital chair, her lips pressed tightly together, blue with anxiety, eyes red, from time to time placing an oxygen mask over his face. My brother never spoke. I could see him doing battle. His eyes had retreated far inside his skull. He had entered a place inside himself, the place I had visited a few years earlier, feverishly communing with dreams and visions, and even possibly ghosts, those hidden parts of ourselves that speak to us using the vocabulary of the dead.

Later, when my brother had returned from hospital and could eventually speak, I asked him about Mr Williams and about standing in front of the metal plates of the X-ray machine. He too had been alarmed at the alacrity of Mr Williams's retreat to the cubicle and the sadness of his demeanour. 'And the white scars on his forehead, as though he had been defenestrated,' said my younger brother with his stupidly advanced vocabulary. 'I know,' I said. 'Though, you know, he fought in the war.' I used the same intonation my father had used, then, with weight and seriousness, added, 'Dunkirk.'

Although seriously ill ('I wondered if he'd make it through the night several times,' says my mother, still shaking at the thought), he did have patches of time where he got out of bed. Then he would build things, rigging up a piece of string from his bedroom to the kitchen with a tin at each end, 'a string telephone', so that he could speak down to my mother and ask for water or a boiled egg. The string went through eyelets and around corners and was a valuable contraption for him as he was able to persecute my mother from a distance with constant demands for lemonade and tea. He read aeroplane and helicopter books, cut out pictures of them and stuck them on his wall, the images of freedom at odds with his own immobility.

Later, when we were adults, I spoke to him about our shared illnesses during our childhoods. We were walking together along the beach at Ynyslas, him striding out on his heels, his long thigh bones outlined against his jeans, sand stretching out across the background, his hair trimmed short, his face set against the sky. It was then that he referred to the strange mist that arose around him one evening as he lay ill in the hospital in Llandrindod. There, he said in his strong, sonorous voice with its Welsh accent floating above the sound of the sea,

'When I was ill I knew I was hovering on the line between life and death. That evening I entered a different space inside myself. It was still and quiet and I realised ...'
What?
'That I could remain alive if I chose to.'
You chose to live?
'No.'
You chose to die?
'Yes.'
I didn't know that.
'Later I awoke.'

I looked at my brother's face, his bright eyes, his dark skin, his direct gaze, his shoulders level, his chest open, his neck up, the sun gleaming upon him. He was brimming with life and his laugh spread along the beach and over the waves.

3.9

We set off back into the traffic, edge through the rest of Bad Oeynhausen, move onto Autobahn 2 towards Berlin. 'Should be there in five or six hours,' says my father.

> By the way.
> *What?*
> Have you taken your pills today?
> *Don't nag. I'm not a child.*
> For your blood pressure and your eyes?
> *Took them both this morning.*

The Autobahn is three lanes wide as we pass Hannover. We stop in a lay-by for the lavatory. It is a small wooden hut, behind which is a field with several horses in it. All are wearing the same burgundy quilted horse blankets, all have their heads low to the ground as they graze. 'Fine horses,' my father says, 'and very well looked after.'

> *I used to look after the horses during the school holidays.*
> Did you?
> *Found them to be good company.*
> You didn't stay with a family during the holidays?

No.

Why not?

Never invited.

We pass windmills, a hundred or so, white and spread out over several miles, some with three blades some with two, some with red stripes on their tips. As we approach the outskirts of Berlin the traffic thickens. We leave Autobahn 2, join the 10, then the 115 then the 100. We make our way along Dominucusstraße, Hauptstraße past Potsdamer Platz with its glass-walled buildings, continue along the wide Leipziger Straße from where we can see the Fernsehturm, the futuristic-in-a-1970s-way-but-now-retro TV mast with its bulbous top, like an onion plant. It is one of the emblems of the old East Berlin and still one of the tallest free-standing structures in Europe. We pass signs to the Spittelmarkt U-Bahn and turn onto Alte Jakobstraße.

Alte Jakobstraße is a street that has low 1950s concrete buildings on one side and building sites on the other. Some of the sites have plywood hoardings around them that are covered in large, optimistic, computer-generated pictures of how the completed buildings will look.

Several articulated lorries are parked in a line. They carry containers, their faded colours familiar from the ferry crossing, salt blue, mud brown, dented, edged with rust. Men in hard hats and fluorescent jackets work on the foundations. They pour cement from a long caterpillar-like tube connected to a large red-and-white industrial cement mixer.

The cement flows quickly into deep plywood-shuttered trenches that have been dug into the surrounding ground. The men's postures are crooked, their bad backs causing them to move in a way that protects the damaged synovial discs that lie between their vertebrae. They kick their feet out as they walk, their steel-capped boots weighting the end of each of their legs.

Mr Bubyage would have loved it here.

Mr Bubyage would have been like a pig in shit.

The Grimm's Hotel is clad in dull panels the colour of zinc. It is tiny. A short strip of carpet has been laid across the narrow pavement outside its front doors. 'They're expecting us,' says my father. 'They've rolled out the red carpet.'

I park the car next to the pavement, walk to the hotel, along the two steps of carpet and through a pair of electric sliding doors into an immaculate but tiny white foyer with two white sofas, each with steel legs. I collect the key for the hotel's car park from reception, return to the car and manoeuvre it into the concrete basement car park. We collect our luggage and take the lift back to reception. I say to the receptionist, as I collect the keys to our room, 'There's a lot of building going on around here.' 'Yes,' he replies, 'the wall passed nearby.' 'But the wall came down twenty-five years ago,' says my father. 'Yes,' replies the man, 'that side of the street was part of no-man's land.' 'Really,' says my father, looking towards it before continuing, 'Lots of Berlin will be part of what was no-man's land.' 'That's true,' replies the man at reception.

I'd spent ages choosing a hotel on the internet, eventually deciding on the Grimm's because of its excellent ratings on TripAdvisor with over 1,500 reviews averaging an 8.9, placing it in the category of 'fabulous'. As well as this, the idea of Grimm's tales appealed to me, with their disturbingly dark and bloody endings, though the atmosphere created by the Brothers Grimm is entirely absent from the hotel foyer's design. Its minimal style contradicts their tales, stuffed with psychological clutter, ruins and physical pain. In fact the Grimm brothers seem to have no purchase on the ambience of this hotel whatsoever. It has been freshly painted white with occasional splashes of lime green on some of its walls. Its floors are polished concrete. Circular, tangerine carpets are laid upon it like stepping stones.

We take the sparkling, mirrored, stainless-steel lift to the fourth floor, catching sight of ourselves in the full-length mirror at the back of the lift. We enter the room. As I swing open the door I am faced with a quote painted in black copperplate upon the emulsion wall in front of me:

'Hertz, was verlangst du mehr?' fragt Hans im Grimm's Märchen. 'Hans im Glück.' Er ist voll und ganz zufrieden, mit sich, seinem Leben und der Welt.

And then on another wall its translation in English:

'Heart, what more can I want?' asks Hans in the Grimm's fairy tale. 'Hans in Luck.' He is very pleased with himself, his life and the world.

'Isn't that extraordinary?' I say. My father looks at the writing, reads it, says nothing and walks into the middle of the room. 'Isn't it weird?' I say.

> *Nothing* weird *about it.*
> But don't you think it's a sign?
> *A sign of what?*
> I don't know what.
> *Why can't you say what you mean?*
> I don't quite know what I mean.
> *You booked us into the Grimm's Hotel. What-did-you-bloody-well-expect?*
> But it mentions your name and says you're in luck. Sometimes inexplicable things happen.
> *You don't know this particular Grimm's story, do you?*
> No, I don't.
> *Thought not.*
> So what is it?
> *A young man called Hans makes a series of bad deals with people but chooses, despite this, to think he's lucky. He starts with a block of gold the size of his own head then he loses everything.*
> He's naïve?
> *Not naïve. Stupid.*

My father places his suitcase on the floor then sits in a chair, his back upright, his legs crossed. I make a cup of tea, boiling the water in the small plastic kettle, pouring UHT milk into my cup from a tiny plastic container. He takes his tea black.

So you looked after horses when you came to Britain?
I did, yes. There were lots of horses when I arrived. It was only when tractors were introduced after the war that horses were taken from the fields.
Working horses?
That's right.
What happened to them?
They were transported to the slaughterhouse. Or ridden there and left. Tied to posts.
How many were killed, do you think?
Millions. Their flesh was used for dog food, their skin for leather, their bones ground into bonemeal, their hooves were melted down for glue.
The countryside must have looked very different then.
It was transformed because all the skills that accompanied them disappeared, too. The farrier, the blacksmith, the wheelwrights, the cartwrights. And the objects too — horseshoes, nails, traces, saddles, bits, reins, all the tackle vanished from the streets of every village and town as though never present.

My father stands and, carrying his tea, walks to the large glass door at the side of the room. He opens it and walks onto the small balcony that overlooks the building sites we have passed. Cold air rushes past us. He gazes across the rough patch of land that used to be 'no-man's land' and then further out at a small section of the city. He looks for some time without saying anything, then turns and walks back into his bedroom, collects his case, leaves the room and closes the door behind him.

3.10

When I was twelve I used to lie awake at night wondering how my father had managed to leave his family, his country and his friends and I realised that I would not be able to survive such a blow. The impossibility of my father's situation often occurred to me at these times and perhaps accounted for my difficulties at school where I learned about none of the important things such as escape, survival, the mental powers necessary for journeying.

Later, as a teenager, I unwittingly began to act out a frail version of my father's escape. I travelled abroad for weeks at a time, refusing to tell anyone where I was going, partly because I did not know myself as I passed through France on trains and coaches into Italy. At some point I was in Malaysia and Thailand, sitting on train roofs, and then Laos, eventually finding myself in the mountains of Myanmar, then Burma, staying in villages with wild dogs and waterfalls to wash in, far away from everyone. As this was before mobile phones, not only did no one know where I was, I didn't know where I was either, as I relentlessly kept moving with only generalised maps to follow.

By my early twenties I had become isolated, partly because I had begun to find it very difficult to converse with people, words just didn't seem to form, and partly because my activities and solitude put people off. At times I felt so lonely that I searched for queues at shops to stand in, hoping they would move slowly so that I could spend some time in close proximity to people who might be chatting amicably and fondly to each other. I found that I could not go to a barber in case I had to talk to the person cutting my hair, so I grew it long. Cafés became a trial in case I had to speak to a waiter. I became more and more reclusive. I lived off fried eggs and earned my living by working in forests and on farms in Wales, England and Scotland, and doing other odd jobs, including, for several months, building and painting a helicopter hangar in the Shetland Islands at Sumburgh airport.

As this hangar was situated within a short walk from Jarlshof, an excavated Stone Age settlement, it meant I could, before and after work, wander around the ancient cylindrical stone buildings whose entrances face directly onto the sea. It was there, at dawn, while sitting on the stone floor of one of the oldest habitations in Europe, that I watched the sun slowly reveal itself, seemingly emerging from the sea. I became aware of the building's sophisticated positioning that allowed me a perfect view of the sunrise from inside its main chamber and so knew I was sitting where others had sat to watch it too, though they had done so thousands of years earlier. At such moments I would force myself to think about my life. I would wonder what it was for and whether it was worth anything. Loneliness gripped me like a virus as I unknowingly but devotedly made my strange pilgrimage towards the echo of my father's past.

Eventually I managed to get a job on Rig 83 on Ninian South in the North Sea. There I felt the elation of storms and the wind driving into my body, the purest air cramming my lungs, the wind driven so quickly into me that it seemed to dissolve my body and at times thrillingly lift my feet off the ground for a second or two, turning me one way then the other in a kind of spirit dance. I learned not to be frightened when this happened but to relax, 'to go with it' and so to experience elation, as though I had drunk an elixir.

Once a gale blew up and I was told to climb the series of three ladders up to the derrick board, which is situated 90ft above the drill floor. This was because the wind had become so strong that, unusually, it was blowing the drill pipe out of the 'fingers' it was being kept in. This meant that the loose drill pipe had started to shake the rig. As a hundred drill pipes, each approximately 90ft long, weigh many tons this was a problem. As Mike, the assistant driller, told me in his Texan drawl: 'A wind like this will blow the drill pipe around so much it'll push the rig over, everyone knows that. It'll have to be tied back.'

Rig 83's drill floor was 400ft above the sea. The climb up the ladder to the derrick board was a further 90ft above this. These steel ladders usually have hoops behind them to stop people falling off, but Rig 83's main ladder was open. As I got to the base of the ladder my hard hat was blown off my head and then, for the first and only time in my life, my glasses too. I realised that I would be blown off this ladder if I climbed it. But because of the photos on the walls of my father's study showing him as the medical officer of the SAS, preparing to parachute into the jungle, and because I could hear his voice encouraging me to 'give it a go', even though one slip would mean certain death, I decided that I would climb it. I worked out the wind direction and decided to climb up one of its edges rather than the normal way. This meant that the wind was behind me, pushing me against the ladder's side.

I remember looking first at one of my hands and then the other as I climbed, noting to myself to move only one limb at a time, never two limbs together. The presence of the wind blowing through me, the colours of the North Sea at night, its surface white with foam, the water raging, vicious and ruthless, the spray hitting me even though I was by now nearly 500ft above the surface, the noise of huge volumes of air hurtling past me and the sense of bleeding into the world while watching my fingers unfurl around each of the ladder's bars before gripping the next one made me exist in the present moment so that all other worries were extinguished. I even resisted the immense temptation to let go to see what would happen, to experience becoming part of the wind and of the storm before dropping into the sea.

When I finally got to the top of the final ladder I clambered onto the area next to the derrick board. This was inside the windbreak, meaning I was protected from the wind. And so as dawn broke over the North Sea, its grey light bleeding all colours pale, spray occasionally hitting me as it leapt over the wind wall, I tied the drill pipe, which was by now bouncing around, back into the rig's fingers, the noise of the rattling pipe a cacophony as metal bashed into metal. Afterwards I tied back a part of the wind wall that was coming loose on the corner of the rig, climbing outside it again so that I felt the wind drive through my back, though by now it was quietening. Afterwards I climbed down the ladders back to the drill floor. The next day I was told that the wind speed had, at times, exceeded the maximum the anemometer could record meaning I had climbed the ladders in what is officially termed a hurricane.

Later I wondered why I needed to do such things. I came to recognise that, although my father and I could not communicate with words, we shared the understanding that while living through extreme moments we realised we wanted to remain alive, that we did not choose death but instead longed for life. These experiences were a balm to the indifferent times of our lives, where being alive or dead seemed to be neither here nor there. Extreme danger provoked in us both the desperate hunger of wanting to be alive.

4.1

The man on reception tells us that Berlin's Jewish Museum isn't far from the hotel, that in fact it's only a twenty-minute walk away. He provides us with a small map that he rips off a roll of paper maps on the reception's counter. He does this with a flourish, his pride in the elegance of his action palpable, as the ripped-off map floats at first up into the air and then down onto the counter before landing directly in front of us. He shows us the route, marking our destination with a cross, digging his pen into the paper, making a long groove along the streets we need to walk down. Encouraged by how close the museum is, and the fact that 'Now at last we have a bloody map', we decide to step out and walk there, my father dressed in fleece-lined gloves, thick waterproof coat, woollen scarf and brown polished shoes that he has just shone using the hotel's rotating-shoebrush machine ('marvellous contraption – could do with one of these at home') situated beside the entrance to the lift.

We set off over the red carpet and onto the street. The wind is sharp this morning, and strong enough to rattle the temporary steel-mesh fencing that surrounds the building sites, the sound of metal rapidly hitting metal a suitable cacophony to accompany us to our destination. There are only a few people on the streets, all dressed in thick clothes, hunkered down, gaze to the ground. The traffic is light. The wind picks up speed on Alte Jakobstraße as it is funnelled between the rows of high buildings on either side, so that for periods of time we must lean our bodies into it. It makes our eyes water, my father's particularly, so that long tears pass down his cheeks. We walk onto Ritterstraße then onto Lindenstraße. Predictably we get slightly lost, and so it takes us an hour to arrive and join the long queue that snakes out from Berlin's Jewish Museum, whose entrance is in a large baroque building, its cream, well-kept walls and high, red-tiled roof a surprise. Security guards are outside, ushering the queue in urgently, their uniforms enlarging and emboldening them, their mouths set straight in a self-conscious display of authority. They seem to be in a rush, almost pushing us through the doors, urging us to move on, then placing our bags through the airport-style X-ray machine. After having our bags checked, we move on to queue again and purchase a ticket. I feel indignant that my father has to pay. Surely he should be privileged, with his own special guide? Surely he is a VIP at this museum? I ask the ticket seller behind his counter if there is a reduction for *Kindertransportees* but he, understandably, declines to engage with the conversation. 'No, there is no reduction for *Kindertransportees*.' Instead, we join the rest of the public as they stand waiting for their own private encounter with the darkness of the material that awaits them. I want to shout out into the foyer, 'Do you know who's here today?'

We drop off our coats and walk towards the staircase that will lead us down to the exhibition. A large glass enclosure is on our left. It has been built between the two wings of the original baroque building and covers what was once a courtyard. To one side of it is a small café. 'I could do with a piece of cheesecake,' says my father, 'and a black coffee. I've got a bit cold and I need the lavatory.' I see the fragility of his hands dancing against his mouth, their blue crinkled veins running over the tops of their sinews, his eyes still watering from the cold during the walk, his bitten nails. 'Of course,' I reply. 'I'd like one too. Let's have a coffee.' We find the toilets together and then return to queue in the café that is small but tastefully decorated and sells no produce with any advertising logos on it. The colour scheme is matt black and cream, and information about prices is written onto the walls in a nod to the design motifs of an imagined Berlin Jewish café of the 1930s. We both choose a black coffee, and eventually, after much deliberation, the blueberry cheesecake rather than the raspberry, which looks equally perfect, even-though-it's-only-ten-thirty-in-the-morning-and-we've-only-just-had-breakfast.

We descend four stone steps into the large courtyard with our illicit, highly calorific comfort food. The courtyard has a high glass canopy above it and we take a seat at a table. The white steel pillars supporting the glass roof high above us are thick and irregular, angled strangely, making an odd, deliberately tortured structure, though the light that falls through the glass panes is inviting, full of flecks and frisky shadows. The uneasy white roof pillars echo the theme of the museum, part of architect Daniel Libeskind's idea that the building housing the records of oppression, murder and erasure should itself suggest confusion, estrangement, anguish, the pillars of witness. The disrupted pillars of the courtyard contrast with the creaminess of the blueberry cheesecake and the dark liquorice coffee we are consuming. Both are fragrant and delicious, the intensity of their flavours providing a moment of childlike pleasure. The sensations are in opposition to the significance of our location. 'Should we even be eating this here?' I think to myself, as the tastes spread through me, unnerving me with their disrespectful frivolity. My father is tucking into his with relish. 'Marvellous cheesecake, absolutely delicious.'

We are surrounded by young people, many accompanied by their teachers, most dressed in bright colours, their spectacle frames various shades of bright plastic, their jeans fashionably ripped, their tops bright primary colours, covered in phrases, their rucksacks all drawn from the same colour chart, magenta or pink or lime, their notebooks and pens busy, moving shards of sky blue or black or luminescent orange, their training shoes branded with various logos – Nike, Adidas, Puma. Collectively they create a sea of colours, like tropical fish in an aquarium, their apparel's colouring, as well as the glow of their youthful skin and lustre of their hair, at odds with the discreet palette of the courtyard's décor, scrubbed red brick, steel and glass, angry white steel pillars, grey stone floor, tables and chairs the colour of slate with black rubber stoppers on each of their feet. My father watches the young people as they mill about, their shifting patterns and constant rearrangements, groups moving around the courtyard in waves, a fluttering of youth. Most are quiet, some are serious, some are laughing quietly and chatting about their full-of-colour lives that have descended today onto the museum of the tortured and murdered. Some have brought their own food and are eating biscuits, drinking brightly coloured smoothies from plastic bottles, sipping cans of drinks, the combination of brands suddenly shriekingly brash and meaningless, the packaging garish. I ask my father,

> Do you think people should be allowed to wear bright
> colours into this museum?
> *They can wear what they like.*
> But all this colour?
> *They're full of life.*
> But don't you think it's disrespectful?
> *I think the opposite. They're here. Life goes on.*

We finish the cheesecake, then walk to the top of the steps that will take us down to the modern extension of Berlin's Jewish Museum, Daniel Libeskind's famous ziggurat that confuses and disorientates the visitor. Below us at the bottom of the stairs we will walk to the exhibits that chart the destruction of the Jewish people of Berlin, of the Jewish people of Germany, of the Jewish people of the whole of Europe. Hidden among it all is the wreckage, destruction and the deaths of my father's family. A crime against humanity; a crime against my father; a genocide. This is the beginning of the piece of architecture with its uneven floors and sloping walls and disorientating route that culminates in a concrete bunker with no escape, a grey chamber with a steel door, the simulacrum of a gas chamber. We walk down three flights of slate steps. My father moves cautiously, his feet slowing as we reach the bottom of the steps, as he turns the corner to the first gallery, whose black slate floor now slopes upwards. He stops and steadies himself, holds onto the anodised metal bannister. He grasps his shoulder.

Are you all right?
I'm fine.
Are you sure you want to do this? We don't have to.
What are you talking about? Of course I want to do it.

I wait for a while as he gathers himself and then we set off up the sloping floors and past the sloping walls. We turn a corner to find a series of picture windows. Behind the glass are displays of everyday objects from the 1930s – some family silver, a pearl broach, a damaged menorah that survived the war and, oddly, a vast syringe the size of a child's arm. Behind these objects there are photographs in black and white showing scenes of Germany during the 1930s – village streets, a crossroads, houses, town shops with signs in them.

The signs are written in amateur, irregular fonts and many underlined: JUDEN! NICHT ERWÜNSCHT!; DIE EINWOHNER-SCHAFT DES ORTES WÜNSCHT KEINEN UMGANG MIT JUDEN; JUDEN SIND UNERBETENE GÄSTE. My father is fascinated by the display. 'Look, that's exactly it, that's what it looked like ... look ...' As he stands in front of the display an energising smile spreads over him. 'I remember it so clearly. All these signs suddenly sprouting up everywhere, all of a sudden. This is how it starts. It starts with signs.' Everyone else who is looking at the exhibits is quiet, many of them the young people in their bright colours from the café, others contemplative couples, but my father is enlivened. 'Look at this! Over here! Look at this sign on that gate.' He points to a picture of a sign above a white wooden gate that says: KEINE JUDEN AUF DIESER FÄHRE ERLAUBT.

> *I remember a sign like this. I was taken on holiday with my mother after my father had died to Hiddensee and there was a ferry and it said on the gate to it, 'No Jews allowed on the ferry', and I said to my mother, 'Look, it says "No Jews",' and she said, 'Be quiet, we're going to walk straight past it, take no notice, we're going on that ferry.' And we did.*
> You just went through?
> *We just walked past.*

We carry on through the exhibition. My father stops and places his hand against a wall. He says,

The photograph of my father's shop after Kristallnacht?

Yes.

Who found it?

Your grandson Freddie found it. It was in the Imperial
War Museum in London in their Holocaust exhibition.

I remember standing inside that shop with my father.

Where was it?

*I can't remember. He had five shops and I can't remember
where any of them were.*

Five?

Yes.

What were they like inside?

Full of handbags, belts, gloves, jewellery, that sort of thing.

What happened to you on the day after Kristallnacht?

I was at home when it happened so I didn't know much about it.

What happened then?

*I attended a non-Jewish school because my mother was a
communist and not at all religious. When I arrived on what
must have been 10 November my friends who were then only
eleven or twelve boasted to me about how they had gone out
the previous night to smash up Jewish shops with their fathers.*

Really?

*And they bragged about how much they had enjoyed smashing
up my father's shop.*

We stand in the air-conditioned air and the artificial light
that casts few shadows. I look at my feet and notice that
one foot is pressed against the other. My finger joints ache.

People move past us. My father clasps his hands together and then pulls himself up. He stands straight:

> *Of course if you've ever been spat on, truly spat on, by a Nazi you know about it. It really is most unpleasant. When I went back to the school there were two Nazis on the stairs, two grown men, and I had to pass them and they both spat at me in my face. They rolled their phlegm in the back of their throats and they spat at me and they more or less soaked me. Then they pushed me down the stairs. It's most unpleasant being spat on by two Nazi adults.*

His face remains smiling but then creases and goes red. But there is no self-pity.

> *Politicians can turn on racism like a tap.*

He suddenly walks to the next exhibit, signalling that this bit of the conversation is now over. And why shouldn't it be?

> *Look, this is about the Nazis insisting that we insert Israel into our names if we were male and Sarah if we were female. All of us had to do it. So officially I became Hans Israel, my sister Toni Sarah and my mother Ruth Sarah.*

We carry on through the museum, passing more exhibits until we come to the concrete chamber. It is entered through a large, heavy steel door. I push it open using both hands. We walk through the doorway. The door closes behind us with a thud. It has a spring on it. We stand in the half-light. It's cold. A small amount of light and an array of unintelligible sounds leak through a small slit at the top of the chamber. Its ceiling is high above us, perhaps 40ft, and painted black. The shape of the room moves to a point at one end. It is a facsimile of a gas chamber. It is made entirely from concrete. It is simplicity itself. The concrete is smooth and has been shuttered using steel plates rather than wood. This is a simulacrum of where some of my father's family died, where his Jewish neighbours and relatives were murdered. He is one of only a few survivors. We bow our heads in silence. We press our hands together.

I stand as still as I can. The sounds from outside are muted. The air surrounding us is grey. My father gazes at the floor. We stay like this for a long time. I want to take a photograph of my father with my phone but stop myself. I must not intrude. Suddenly the large metal door swings open and some of the chattering young people enter. They do not lower their voices or decrease the velocity of their movements or look at us. Even when the steel door closes harshly behind them, symbolically locking them in, they continue to chatter. Their body language is effervescent, full of inquisitive pleasure, their conversation animated, their outfits seemingly even more resplendent in this mono-chrome world of shadows, the movements of their feet and elbows a concerto of life. Perhaps they are affected but it's difficult to tell. More young people enter through the door, from Italy now and Sweden and from France, as well as Germany, Japan and Bulgaria, all these young people talking, some muted, some loud, all in their coloured clothes and trainers, the metal door opening then closing with a bang, some leaving quickly others taking in the silence. My father raises his head, looks up and stares fixedly at them. We are standing at the back wall of the chamber. Then the young people leave and we are alone. The air is colder, the sounds deadened. My father hangs his head again. I think about taking a photograph with my phone again. I know the act of sliding it out of my pocket will break the sanctity of the moment, but I do it. It feels wrong to record this moment, for the recording I know depletes the moment I am recording, but I do it anyway, for the record, for myself. I need to, I must. I take the photograph while he gazes at the floor. There. It's done.

We stay for a little longer and then leave, walking back out through the metal door and out of the chamber. We climb a long flight of stairs to some of the other exhibits, documents and photographs. There is a documentary film about Berlin made in 1929 entitled *Menschen am Sonntag* (People on Sunday), showing people happily walking through the city, directed by, among others, Billy Wilder before he moved to Hollywood, became an American and directed *Double Indemnity* and *Some Like It Hot*. In *Menschen am Sonntag*, people flirt and small happinesses are recorded. No one has any understanding of what is to come. How can they? We pass more documents about selections, photographs of Bergen-Belsen, records of train movements, pictures of Auschwitz, photographs of the *Einsatzgruppen* murdering my Jewish compatriots at point-blank range with rifles.

We watch a short documentary made during the 1960s in Germany about the prosecution of Nazi leaders in the 1950s. We listen to Hannah Arendt, who coined the term 'the banality of evil' during Adolf Eichmann's trial in Jerusalem, meaning that evil could occur through a series of discrete, banal-seeming actions – the driving of a train, the distribution of clothes, the making of paths, the sorting of banknotes, the insertion of a gas canister outside a chamber. On their own these actions were nothing, but joined together they allowed the Holocaust. Hannah Arendt leaps out of the screen in black and white. 'This should not have happened,' she states in her thrilling smoker's voice, her mouth articulate, her energy vibrating the monitor. 'We all have enemies, we accept that. And why not? Who of any substance does not have enemies?' she declares, before adding, 'But always there has been a way of politically solving things and moving on, always it has been possible.' She stops, the grain of the black-and-white film leans into the future, her eyes are bright stones. 'But this,' she asserts, 'is the abyss.'

When the film finishes we make our way back to the café. We move slowly. The air of the world is thick again. My father's body is weighted down, his knees don't quite bend properly. He shuffles. 'I'll just have a coffee,' he says. 'You can forget the raspberry cheesecake' – referring, presumably, to a debate he has been having with himself but which he hasn't voiced. I collect two coffees and we sit together in another part of the café that is inside the original building. Here there are tables with grey-and-white gingham tablecloths and cushions laid on wooden benches painted the colour of anthracite. He is still silent. For a long time he does not speak. Things percolate through him. How brave he has been. What magnificence. To survive what he has survived and then to make this visit. He has the heart of a lion. He has the strength of a bull. Grace surrounds him.

He looks up at the people who are returning from their visit around the museum. A delicate woman with a small pointed nose, gold wire-rimmed glasses and a white cheesecloth shirt sits with her black-bearded son in silence, staring into the middle distance. A young man with a shaved head and thick black glasses walks past us with a large piece of apple pie on his plate that has a mountain of cream on its top, which he slowly and carefully eats with a fork, a morsel at a time. A young woman wearing an emerald sarong and long, glittering earrings enters with her partner, a man with a pierced nose and grey floral trousers. They sit quietly, eyes locked. Two young students arrive, texting on their phones. All are quiet, hushed.

Suddenly the silence is disrupted. Music is playing just behind a door. I see one of the waiters dancing. He is lean and fit. His hips move gently and slowly in circles, his fellow waiters watch and laugh. His arms are raised, held high, a radiance, an eroticism. My father smiles at the flirtation.

Isn't it marvellous that all these people come and visit this place of all places? That such a place exists. That it is full of life? In here. Of all places.

I go to the counter and ask who the music is by. 'Pharrell Williams, "Happy",' the waiter tells me with a smile. The music is playing from his phone. The sound is tinny. I get more coffee and we move back into the courtyard to sit. The young people begin to arrive after their visit to the exhibits, their body movements slower than earlier, their chatter quieter. Gradually the air of the courtyard becomes a low buzz of conversation. Their colours begin to teem across the floor again, through the warm heated air. My father is pale and still. The emotions are coming to get him. The dogs are at his heels. I can see it on his face. He looks towards me and through me, and so beyond me. I see his mind spinning and whirling. He starts to say something but then he shuts his eyes, his mouth falls open slightly, sagging to one side. He is grey with tiredness. He places his head back and sleeps, uncomfortably, his head resting to one side on his dark chair in this steel and glass courtyard with its thick, strong, tortured pillars, its beautiful young people.

4.2

For our summer holidays we would camp in the small town of Dale in Pembrokeshire on the west coast of Wales, my father towing his tiny home-made dinghy, *Sal*, behind us on a trailer. Dale is situated on the edge of a large sheltered bay. To the south lies a headland, St Ann's Head, beyond which lies the Irish Sea. Each year leaflets were given out warning people not to sail a dinghy beyond St Ann's Head for two reasons. The first was that the swell was much larger and far more unpredictable beyond the headland's protection; the second was because oil tankers sailed past it in order to dock at the deep-water port of Milford Haven. There their oil was pumped directly to the newly constructed refinery through which nearly a third of the UK's annual oil supply was unloaded. The proximity of the oil refinery to the port was linked to the recent development of supertankers that had started to come into service, tankers so large that they could carry millions of gallons of crude oil. These tankers took twenty minutes to come to a stop and their hulls pushed out a huge wake. It was this that was particularly dangerous to dinghies. As the leaflets noted, 'It can easily capsize a small vessel.' As well as this, supertankers have very large propellers or screws that, as my father explained, 'are so powerful that if you go too near to the oil tanker's stern the current caused by the propellers drags a dinghy under the sea's surface'.

Perhaps because of these warnings my father always sailed as close as he could to any of these supertankers. 'What an incredible vessel,' he would shout out as we sailed directly towards one of their matt-black hulls. 'It's colossal!' he would carry on. 'It carries over 2 million gallons of oil! Two million gallons! Let's get a closer look.' To his delight some of them would sound their horns to warn us away. 'Did you hear that?' he would shout laughingly as the sound waves crossed the water.

I was seven when I was taken sailing, and at that age I couldn't swim. Although I wore a life jacket I knew that if I fell into the sea I would drown. This is because I had to wear thick woollen jumpers to keep warm and these would fill with water if I fell out of the boat or it capsized. I knew this because my father kept telling me, 'Don't fall in, those jumpers will fill with water and drown you.'

Just as he relished the adventure of sailing in his home-made boat, the waves crashing over us, the boat needing urgent bailing out with a small plastic bucket used to make sandcastles, the violent swings and turns of the sail, the cold Welsh salt air turning my fingers blue, so I dreaded it. Where I was terrified if a large wave hit us, he was exhilarated and would call out to me with a huge grin, his hair dancing around his eyes in the wind, 'This is the life.' As I clung to the sheet and the spray stung my eyes, he would squeal with pleasure. 'This is the life,' he would repeat, as I held onto the jib, not daring to look over the boat's edge. Where the freedom of the ocean enchanted him, I felt its deep water under me.

Although he would promise my mother that he would not sail beyond the protection of St Ann's Head, he always did so and as soon as we passed its shelter the dinghy would be tossed up and down in a frenzy, for we were now far out in the Irish Sea. Then I would watch my father concentrating intently, his eyes alert to the movement of waves and wind, his hands locked onto the tiller, flicking it one way then the other, his arm pulling at the mainsail while he shifted his body to stabilise the boat. 'It's wild out here,' he would shout against the backdrop of the noise of the sea and the splash of the boat's hull pushing through the water. 'That was a wave,' he would exclaim gleefully as we were both soaked by water breaking over us. Suddenly, if he needed to change direction he would bellow, 'Ready about!' followed by, 'Lee-ho!' As he issued this instruction he would move the tiller rapidly from one side of the boat to the other, so making the boom lurch rapidly across its deck. As the boom shot towards me I would quickly duck my head as low as I could, feeling its rush as it skimmed my head, and then crawl onto the other side of the boat. 'Remember you must duck low or the boom will either knock you unconscious or into the sea. Or both.'

During these trips we fished for mackerel by hanging a string of fishing hooks with brightly coloured feathers attached to them from the back of the boat. I would throw these feathers overboard then periodically look for fish. 'Check the feathers,' my father would say, 'bob them up and down.' I would do as I was told, watching the feathers' colours fanning out below the waves until eventually we caught a mackerel. I could feel it pulling against me along the fishing line, experiencing the intimate connection between hunter and prey, between killer and about-to-be-killed, each twist and turn, each thrash felt through the fishing line in the palm of my hand. Mackerel fight and writhe in a frenzy; their whole bodies thrash against the hook that has passed through their mouths. They fight to their death. I would watch them struggle for life just below the surface before I pulled them out of the water, their astonishing colours, purple and mauve and green, radiating under the surface and then reflecting brightly in the sharp air.

As I pulled the fish out of the water they became much heavier and began to thrash even more violently. As soon as my father realised I had a mackerel on the end of the line he would turn the boat so that its bow faced the direction the wind was blowing from. 'We're going into the wind,' he would shout, 'so that the boat remains stationary.' He would turn the boat rapidly and loosen the sails, which consequently flapped uncontrollably, the sound of them suddenly deafening. The swell of the Irish Sea lifted us up one moment and down another, while the smaller surface waves covered the boat with spray. After I landed the fish my father would quickly grab it, tear the hook out of its mouth, take up one of the rowlocks, the large lumps of Y-shaped metal that the oars rest in, and, while holding the fish's body against the edge of the boat, start to hit it violently until dark blood oozed from its pulverised head, the boat rocking madly one way then the other at each hit, the fish wriggling for some time before dying. Then my father would throw each mackerel into the bottom of the boat, his teeth clenched in his familiar grimace. He would repeat the process as each fish was caught, hitting them until their heads were flat while cursing them if they escaped from his hands. 'Come here, you little bastard,' he would shout, as the boat rocked wildly and the fish thrashed about. 'Come here you little fucker.' Occasionally we would catch twenty or so mackerel. All would be dealt with in the same way, the sound of the heavy metal hitting the flesh of the fish like a damp clump, my father screaming at each fish as it lay on the edge of the boat, its dark blood spattering the varnished boat's wooden hull, its scales iridescent, angelic rivulets of purple, mauve, deep green and brown, the colours from the dead bodies luminous and dancing in a pile at the bottom of the boat.

Some fish fought so hard that they managed to jump out of my father's hands. Slippery and strong and like the cockroaches on the kitchen floor, they escaped to freedom, their bodies flying for a second through the air before returning to the safety of the brine. But most were killed and lay with their bashed-in heads and accusatory eyes staring at me for the rest of the journey across the bay, my father informing me,

You have to be prepared to kill the food you want to eat.

Eventually we returned to land. Then I would walk slowly across the beach feeling the sand's pressure on the soles of my feet, any stone that pushed itself into my arch a welcome stab of pain that reminded me I was safe. I would lie down and stare at the sky and shut my eyes until I could hear a sound that arose from inside me and that passed out through me, emanating from me. It was a long, soothing note and it enveloped me and seemed to connect me to all around me: the sea where I had come from, the seagulls chasing each other through the air as they called, the shimmering scales of the dead mackerel, the small rippling waves as they hit the shore, the sound of people playing on the beach and, it seemed, of the blue sky, its wind and the turning earth. It was the hum that arrived from inside me when I was overwhelmed with relief, the heightened state that occurred when I survived danger and so felt a blessing and so could feel the angelic threads of my heart. As I lay there with the air blowing through my skin and the stones of the beach pressing into my back, the colours of the world glowed.

Later, as the long summer's sun stretched our shadows into our own accompanying giants, and as it began to disappear below the horizon and the beach cooled, we would gather driftwood and make a fire. My father showed us how to lay it properly, finding the lee of the wind for its best location, arranging it first with dried grass, then twigs and then larger pieces of wood and finally logs, all with plenty of air between them so the fire could draw enough oxygen to feed it. He would monitor each piece of wood we brought to him. 'It has to be bone dry,' he would say. 'See if you can find another piece.' When it was built he would light each of its four corners, the dry grass catching immediately and crackling and rapidly turning black as white smoke rose from it, the flames tiny at first, no bigger than a glimmer, before spreading to the smaller wood and then the larger. As the fire overcame its initial timidity and began to take and then blaze, he would show us how to gut the mackerel with the penknife he carried on his key ring. This penknife had a leather handle and was one of his most prized possessions. He had had it since arriving in England and would occasionally sharpen it outside the back door of our house using a long, dark-grey gritstone, patiently pressing and drawing the blade back and forth along the stone through a pool of oil.

Each of us would take it in turns to slice open a fish's stomach, taking care to push this small, lethal knife away from our bodies as we cut into it. He showed us the point where we should cut into the fish's belly, how to pull out the shining pink intestines and float bladders and occasionally the fish's roe and place them in a small bucket for the seagulls. Later, after the fire had heated up and created embers, we would wrap each mackerel in silver foil and throw it into the centre of the fire, later pulling them out with a stick. The foil was covered in ash and we would brush it off and peel it back and find the baked fish inside. They tasted as good as any fish can, these fresh mackerel, baked in their own juices in a fire on the beach, their squashed and battered heads still on the end of their spines.

And I would gaze at the sea and marvel at how far we had sailed only a few hours earlier. I would watch the tankers moving sedately in the distance, now appearing tiny and unthreatening, and would hear the hum again from inside my body.

4.3

We are sitting reading in the hotel when my father announces that he would like to visit the house he used to live in.

I want to visit the house where I was born.

You've never been back?

No.

Why not?

Never wanted to.

You've never looked for your old house before?

After the war my mother moved to East Berlin – you know that. The house I grew up in was in West Berlin.

So you couldn't visit it with her?

Correct.

Where was it?

Near the Tiergarten. To the north. Near the Englischer Garten.

Do you know the address?

Helgoländer Ufer.

I ask the man at the hotel's reception if he could show me where Helgoländer Ufer is. He shows me on one of his paper maps. 'You will need to take a taxi to get there,' he tells me. 'It is quite some distance away.' I turn to my father,

We'll need to take a taxi.

Nonsense.

It's quite far away.

No it isn't.

The man on reception said it was.

I could do with the walk.

It's cold.

We'll have to keep moving, then.

So we walk. First from the hotel to the Spittelmarkt, then down some steps alongside the Spreekanal. My father's spirits lift as he moves to the place where the canal passes underneath a bridge, the Grünstraßenbrücke.

> *We used to watch the tugboats lower their funnels in order to pass under this bridge. Came here with my friends. Their funnels were hinged at their base. They were bent backwards to get under the bridge. Used to stand on the bridge as they passed underneath us. We got covered in steam.*

He stands looking at the bridge. I see his body relax as the memory holds him. A smile spreads across his face. He and his friends waving from the bridge. The tugboat men lowering the tall funnel, guiding the boat. Clouds of steam.

We turn from the canal, walk down the length of Leipziger Straße, with its fast-moving traffic, to Potsdamer Platz and then enter the Tiergarten from its south-eastern corner. There are very few people in the park; most of those who are there are walking their dogs, a few are riding bikes, all are dressed in thick layers of clothes. The park is carefully maintained, dotted with small ponds, low hedges and paths that lead off at surprising angles with statues of historic Prussians – Field Marshal Helmuth Graf von Moltke, an Amazon on horseback in bronze, a series of four large black statues showing the catching of a fox and the killing of a boar. We walk until the cold from the ground passes through my shoes and tickles the soles of my feet. We come to the Englischer Garten.

> *I learned to ride a bike around here somewhere.*
> It's a nice place to learn.
> *It was.*

We walk past the wintering flowerbeds of roses with their pruned and thorny stems, then leave the Tiergarten and walk to the nearby Bellevue S-Bahn station, which my father wants to have a look at. We enter the station past two large flower stalls full of mixed bouquets, as well as single cut flowers in white vases. We climb the station's staircase to the platform. My father gazes at the glass and steel roof.

Always liked this roof. Stock brick walls strengthened with piers. Roof spans made from wrought iron. Large areas of plate glass in the roof. Old building practices and new building practices combined.

I look up at the roof.

This is where I caught the train to Friedrichstraße station to leave Berlin.
This is where you left from?
My mother and I came here to catch a train to Bahnhof Friedrichstraße. I said goodbye to my mother there.
You stood on this platform with your mother?
Yes.
And this is the first time you've been back to this spot?
Yes.
Did Toni come with you? To say goodbye?

My father glances at me. For a split second his eyes look directly into mine. He turns and walks up the platform. An S-Bahn train arrives. A few people board and several others leave. I see their faces change for a fraction of a second as they concentrate on the way the balance of their bodies is about to alter as they step from the edge of the railway carriage onto the platform a few inches below them. I walk to the end of the platform and stand next to Hans. He looks at me and says,

Toni wasn't there.

He turns and walks back down the platform, then down the station steps. By the time I draw level with him he is standing next to the flower stall, among an array of sunflowers and roses, their vivid yellows and scarlets out of time with the cold of autumn. A white tiled wall behind them.

Why wasn't she there?

She just wasn't.

She came to see us in Wales and then we went to Ynyslas with her. Do you remember?

Of course I remember.

Then we never saw her again.

Because she never came to see us again.

But you never went to see her in Israel.

I was very busy.

And when she died you didn't go to her funeral.

My father turns away from the flower shop and moves out into the street and begins to walk off. I catch him up.

I don't want to talk about it.
All right.
I want a coffee.
Me too.
We'll go over there.
Where?
There.

I look into the distance to the other end of the street where he is pointing and see what looks to me, from here, like a large house or possibly a small hotel.

Are you sure that's a café?
Let's try it, shall we?

We walk down Holsteiner Ufer and cross the road. I feel that the cold has moved through my coat and is approaching my bones. The building my father is walking towards has a sign written in red on one of its walls – BAUMKUCHEN SEIT 1852. As we get closer I see that it is a café, the G. Buchwald Konditorei.

166

We walk through the front door to find ourselves in front of a floor-standing cabinet displaying a selection of ornate cakes. Four waiters serve the people queuing, all of them describing each cake in soft, attentive tones: '*Dieser Schokoladenkuchen ist perfekt. Es hat frisch Sahne in Schichten.*'

Through a door I can see a room full of tables. My father walks directly in and sits at a table by a window. Each table in this café has a blood-red tablecloth draped over it. A small white lily in a cut-glass vase has been placed on each tabletop. The walls are patterned with shining silver-beige Anaglypta wallpaper and each chair is covered in an ornately embroidered cloth of buttercream and red oxide. A large flower display rests on an old oak chest at the back of the room. It has South African 'hot pokers' in it. A young, clean-shaven waiter arrives. My father, without looking at him, orders,

Zwei Kaffee schwarz. Zwei Baumkuchen.

The waiter takes the order.

> What's a Baumkuchen?
> *Wait and see.*
> How did you know this was here and what to order?
> *Isn't it obvious?*
> Not really.

The Baumkuchen arrives. It's a piece of multi-layered chocolate cake covered in bitter chocolate. The sponge is light, slightly salty and full of vanilla.

> *I used to come here as a child.*
> You came here?
> *Yes.*
> With your family?
> *Yes.*

He points through the window of the café to a block of apartments 100 metres away. It is six or seven storeys high. Its walls have been painted a dark ochre, the window frames white.

You see those flats?
The dark-coloured ones?
That's where I grew up. We lived on the first floor. The windows on the left are ours.
You lived there?
Yes.
And Toni?
What about her?
What happened between you and her?
Shut up about Toni.

We drink the coffee and finish the cake in silence. The clientele of the café speak softly to each other. I read a leaflet that is printed in English:

The Baumkuchen or Treecake is a finely layered butter cake that has been the speciality of the Buchwald Pastry for 163 years and even today all our Baumkuchen specialities are made using the original recipe from 1852 ... The business relocated to Berlin at the end of the nineteenth century.

For a second I envy the continuity. I sense what my father was excluded from.

We finish the cake and leave. In the café's entrance, next to the cakes in their chilled display cabinet, is an array of certificates that celebrate the awards won by the Buchwald café over the years. Tucked inside an alcove, and partially hidden behind a long floor-to-ceiling curtain of cream cloth, a sign tells us that the café won awards for its cakes in 1942 and 1943. I wonder who the judges were.

We walk out, pass over the Moabiter Brücke, the bridge that passes over the Spree. There are four statues of bears, two at each end of the bridge.

We walk across the bridge, turn right onto Helgoländer Ufer and stop outside his old apartment.

The handle is the same.

He touches it and then so do I. We stand beside each other for some time. A man emerges through the door of the apartments and walks up the street. He's wearing a Breton sweatshirt under a dark raincoat. I take in the view, the bridge, the river, people going about their daily lives. A young mother and her son leave the building and meet the man who left a minute ago, who is returning holding a newspaper next to his Breton shirt. They chat for a minute and he then goes back into the building and the young mother and son walk up the street. A woman, probably in her eighties, comes out through the doors of the building, walking with two sticks. My father stops her and asks if he could look into the foyer, as there is a painting on its wall that he'd like to see. He explains the situation in careful German. The woman is wearing bright-red lipstick and is heavily made up. She is wearing glasses with gold wire frames and lenses with a heavy yellow tint, the tint that is meant to cheer you up. She's dressed in tweeds and she says in English and particularly firmly,

No. We can't let people like you in.

The door closes. She walks slowly up the street. We stay for a while, then leave.

What an unkind woman.
You really can't blame her for not letting us in. She doesn't
know anything about us. I'd like to go to the aquarium.
It's not far.

We move slowly back across the bridge, past the bears
and the Konditorei café, past Bellevue station, past the
Englischer Garten.

It's a lovely area you grew up in.
Except if you were a Jew, yes.

We cross the park and walk to the aquarium. Built in
1913, it has also survived the war. 'I loved this place,' my
father says. 'I used to come here with my friends.' We walk
through its entrance up several steps, buy tickets and wander
around the aquarium's three floors, past insects on logs,
past pale sharks in enormous tanks, past white catfish and
dark-blue eels, past the vivid colours of tropical fish, until
he stands in front of a tank devoted to jellyfish. He watches
them as they move through the water, billowing serenely
as they move in soporific circles around the glass-fronted
tank, suspended it seems in a sort of bliss. Beside the tank
a sign tells us that:

Certain types of jellyfish need to be fed with small pieces
of fish by hand. The food is placed on the jellyfish tentacle
using tweezers or is injected with a cannula into the tentacle

connected to the jellyfish's mouth. Different types of jellyfish should not be placed together as the weaker species would ultimately be eaten by the others.

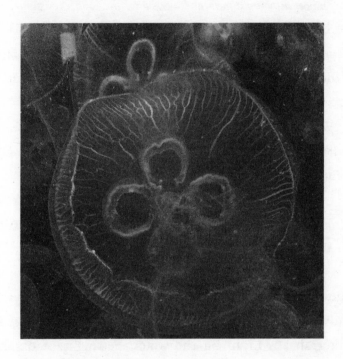

My father is transfixed by the jellyfish.

Toni left to work in Holland shortly before I was put on the
Kindertransport. *She got a job as a maid.*
Your mother chose you?
Things aren't that simple.
Is that what Toni was telling you in Wales?
No it was not.
She was agitated about something.

She was eighteen. I was twelve. That's how the decision was reached.

How did she survive?

She got a job on a farm and worked for the Dutch resistance. She was blonde. She didn't look stereotypically Jewish. At the end she was hidden in a barn by the farmer. When the war finished she took trains to Nice and got on a ship to British Mandated Palestine.

What happened then?

She joined a kibbutz – Ramat Rachel. When the ship arrived at Jaffa it couldn't reach the shore so she dived off the ship and swam to it.

That's what you were talking about?

Yes.

Images of dunes flood me. The sea at Ynyslas. Toni's eyes and her advice. I see her diving off the ship and swimming in the Mediterranean. Light on the water. Setting foot on shore. Heated sand in her toes. Eyes ablaze.

My father, still staring at the jellyfish, says,

She was lucky.

He pauses before continuing.

And so was I.

4.4

It is summer. It's the year 2000. We are in the grounds of Killerton House, a National Trust property situated in Devon. We have been on holiday for a few days – my father, my mother, my wife Barbara and our three young children Joe, Freddie and Rosa. On our return home my father has said he'd like to stop at Killerton House 'to have a look round'.

When we arrive he tells me, while my children are running around the gardens, that this is where he was sent a few weeks after he first arrived in England from Berlin. The boarding school he was sent to attend, Vinehall, was evacuated here during the war and it is here that he began his new life. The mechanics of why and how this happened are unknown to him and, even though he has tried to find out, all he knows is that he was sponsored on the understanding that the sponsor remained anonymous: 'The gift of a stranger.'

He then collects his grandchildren and takes them on a tour, answering their questions. 'This is the staircase I ran up and down'; 'This is where we ate'; 'This is the pantry'; 'This is where I first arrived'. Areas of the property have been cordoned off by the National Trust and so are out of bounds. This means that, as we're with my father, we'll have to walk under these cordons, which we do. We walk into a garage situated near the house. Painted on one of its white walls in black paint are the outlines of woodworking tools – saws, bradawls, screwdrivers, hammers. The method ensures that tools are stored in a way that makes them easy to find. The building hasn't been disturbed for many years. 'I drew those,' says my father. We stand, my children and I, and look at them. This is the first physical proof of his time in England. He tells me there was another Jewish boy who had also come from Germany and had also escaped on the *Kindertransport*.

> That must have been comforting, having someone else
> in the same predicament.
> *We never spoke about it.*
> Did you speak German to each other?
> *No.*
> Not at all?
> *Neither of us mentioned it.*

We leave the stable and walk to the gardens and stand under a tulip tree.

> *After I heard Winston Churchill's speech on the radio declaring*
> *that Britain was at war I walked out into this garden and I*
> *stood exactly here, under this tulip tree. It's here that I realised*
> *that I wasn't going to return to Berlin, that I was going to*
> *remain here in Britain. That's when I realised.*
> What did you realise?
> *That I wouldn't see my mother or my family again.*

Did you know that then?

Yes, I did.

That you'd lost them?

Yes.

And you were twelve?

I'd recently turned twelve, yes. And then I realised something else.

What?

That I was lucky.

Lucky?

Lucky.

I am next to my children who fill me with their life and I understand again what I know already – that he has lived in a different world to the rest of us. He has been set apart. On the surface he appears identical but although he is set within the world, he does not fit into it. He does not move around it easily, does not know how to settle back into it, does not understand how to occasionally float on its gentle surface or, opening his pores, bleed into its grace. Instead, my father fights, hard, desperate, needing to remain in it, wondering if at any moment he will be removed from it.

For him, incessant running and cycling and swimming and gardening and working are things achieved, all these things done; all his adventures tell him what he needs to be reminded of – that he is alive. For him, aliveness is a reckoning of achievements, a list of accomplishments. He knows he's alive because his mind can work this fact out through a process of deduction. He knows he did such and such, visited so and so, ran this many miles, built this shed, cut down this hedge, went there, bought a new mower, did this to that, did that to this, so he can say to himself reasonably confidently that he is alive. This mental processing requires enormous quantities of stimulation. Stillness is impossible.

You were really left in a flat on your own?
Yes
For how long?
Couple of weeks
Could you speak English?
Not really. It was quite funny. I became very frightened of a particular van that drove around. It had the words 'Family Butchers' written on the sides. I thought this was a van full of people who went round butchering families. Then one day someone brought me here.
Where did you go during the school holidays?
Nowhere. I just stayed here. No one seemed to mind. I built a bridge to the island on the lake.

In the distance there is a small lake, which has a bridge to an island in its centre.

I built that, though I'm sure it's been repaired or replaced by now.
That's amazing.
All I know was that it was heaven here.

He pauses before looking at me again.

It was bliss.

His pain as he recalls his memories surrounds me then settles inside me. It moves into my abdomen. It moves under my ribs. I have infused a part of his history; why, I do not know. It has become the dark ghost inside me. I do battle with it but it has gripped me. It is the lining of my heart. It is the stones of my kidneys. It is my arthritic hands. It clings to my vital organs and makes continual battle with my mind, my strange mind that races and cascades its thoughts into me, despite my continual pleas for quiet; incessant pictures, an inherent noise, like the chattering waterfalls in the Welsh hills of my childhood as they spill their water into the wide pools below.

4.5

We move up to the higher floors of the Aquarium. We cross a small bridge above the alligators, their hooded eyes locked into the middle distance, their jawlines millions of years old. We gaze at them and then suddenly my father wants to leave. We exit onto the pavement next to the traffic speeding by on Budapester Straße and start to drift back towards the Tiergarten.

Suddenly my father stops, turns, walks purposefully along the street and crosses the dual carriageway. I follow him. 'Where are we going?' I ask. 'To KaDeWe,' says my father. 'I've remembered something. It's near the KaDeWe.' He begins to walk faster. We push through a set of aluminium doors into a 1960s shopping centre, the Europa-Center, the building that has the large neon Mercedes Star turning on the top of its twenty-storey roof. It's located next to the bombed-out remains of the Kaiser Wilhelm Memorial Church, known as '*der hohle Zahn*' ('the hollow tooth'), which was destroyed by Allied bombing in 1943, its broken roof and pockmarked walls a painful but now glamorous reminder of the Second World War. I think of Bryn Lewis and my father talking at the end of our garden in Pentrosfa.

The Europa-Center claims 'To Provide a Totally New Kind of Shopping Experience', though how it intends to do this is not at all clear We pass two large adverts with smiling models on them, their perfectly aligned capped teeth gleaming in the interior strip lighting: FÜR SNEAKER FREAKS-BIS-HIGH HEELS TRÄGER and FÜR ALTBERLINER BIS NEU-NEUKÖLLNER. We stride under the posters and, as the Europa-Center is tiny, out of the other side in a minute, having had no new kind of shopping experience whatsoever. We turn left and walk along Tauentzienstraße for five minutes, cross the dual carriageway and carry on walking. On our right is a huge department store built at the turn of the twentieth century. 'That's the KaDeWe,' says my father, 'the Kaufhaus des Westens.'

He pushes through the glass doors of the largest department store in continental Europe. I follow. A man in uniform wearing a top hat tilts his head in welcome. We walk into the large atrium inside the entrance. We inhale the perfumes around the make-up counters, pass bars of soap, jars of face creams, eyeliners and lipsticks; walk past watches in small glass cases, see the glimmering crowds.

Bloody nonsense.
What is?
All this – shopping.
It's what people like to do.
Madness.
I don't think I ever once went shopping with you, ever.
Better things to do.
Though your father owned shops.

My father gives me one of his looks.

It's number six.

He turns around on his heel and flies out of KaDeWe, passing the man who has only just nodded to us on our way in, as well as the flood of people arriving at the store. He emerges onto Tauentzienstraße at high speed, walks straight off the pavement into the dual carriageway, waving his arms towards the traffic as he does so, ignores the blaring of horns as he zigzags across the road, allowing lorries and vans to pass either side of him, his hands signalling drivers to let him through. I follow him. We reach the opposite pavement. We walk rapidly for a short time back up Tauentzienstraße, dodge slow-moving shoppers, lovers, fashionistas, him peering into shop windows until he stands in front of one which is a building site.

This must be it. This is the one in the photograph. Number six. Number six. He always talked about number six. Of course it's number six.

Number six Tauentzienstraße is being rebuilt. It is covered in scaffolding and screened by metal mesh fencing. Through this mesh I can see men wearing hard hats and covered in dust, some leaning against a stack of plywood, others looking at a set of plans. The shop is having a major refit.

This is it. This is one of my father's shops. Let's go in.

We can't. It says no entry. Those men won't let us in.
We'll come back in ten minutes then.

We walk back along Tauentzienstraße, take in its wide
carriageway, the density of people, its line of market stalls.
Then we walk back again to number six. The men have
left, or at least they can't be seen. Between two of the mesh
screens is a small gap that has been left for the workers to
get in and out of. We squeeze through this gap, then under
some scaffolding, pass signs saying NO ENTRY and ACHTUNG
and LEBENSGEFAHR! BETRETEN VERBOTEN and stand inside
my grandfather's shop. The walls have been stripped back,
revealing their original concrete structure, built using
wooden shuttering. There is a high window at the back of
the shop. We walk towards it. 'I remember this view very
clearly,' says my father, as we stand together looking out at
a large square, which shops and houses back onto and which
is filled with shrubs and trees.

My father used to lift me up to look out of this window.
You stood here with your father?
We stood here together.

Suddenly I feel faint. My head begins to spin quite violently.
There seems to be a pressure on my forehead. I feel I'm
going to be sick.

I'm sorry, I feel faint.

My father does not reply but paces around and disappears around a corner and then, slightly worryingly, up a long curved staircase. When he's out of sight I lie down on the floor on my front. I feel the pressure come upon my back again. I press my face into the floor. The concrete dust is bitter and dry in my mouth and it eddies up my nose. It sticks to my skin. I taste the floor, kiss it. I stand up and my father rejoins me.

What's all this bloody lying down?
Not quite sure.
It's odd.
I know.
You're covered in dust.
I suppose I am.
There was a counter over here and the goods were arranged in glass cases over here. I often served people.
And your mother?
Sometimes she came with us; usually she stayed at home.
And Toni?
Yes, she came with us too.
The four of you in this shop?
Correct.
Happy?
Happy? I suppose so.

I take a photograph of the construction site in what was my grandfather's shop.

A man emerges dressed in steel-capped boots and a hard hat and with a belt of tools around his waist. He's covered in a thin layer of concrete dust and is both huge and hugely displeased. I can see this from the way his feet are placed in front of me and the way his arms are folded, as well as his direct and intimidating stare. He's in his late fifties, powerfully built, having clearly worked for many years in the construction industry. When I look more carefully at his eyes I see that he is caught between anxiety, embarrassment and fury and that our presence is deeply uncomfortable for him. His eyes look both sensitive and violent, as though he wants to hit me but is pleading with me not to make trouble. He speaks in German, words to the effect that I should leave immediately. I show him my phone and tell him I'm taking a photograph. 'No photographs,' he replies. I look around to see that my father has disappeared. I can't see him. But the man is insistent and asks me to leave, pointing to the shop's entrance. When I do leave, I find my father already standing on the pavement. He's quiet but not at all shaken. We stand together for some time, looking at the shop. I try to find the closest position that the Kristallnacht photograph was taken from, but can't get close because of the building works.

We walk back to the Grimm's Hotel where my father tells me before sleeping that tomorrow he would like to visit his father's grave and his grandfather's grave in Weißensee, 'for the first time in my life'.

4.6

The jumble sales in Llandrindod had raffles with prizes of Mateus rosé and Blue Nun wines and coach trips to Aberystwyth, as well as large tins of biscuits and cardboard boxes full of meat from Abberley, the butcher. Often the town's silver band played at the side of the hall or on the stage, its harmonious music warming the hall; 'Nimrod' from Elgar's *Enigma Variations*, Viennese waltzes, the theme from *The Dambusters*, as well as military marches. One corner of the hall was always occupied by elaborate cakes: coffee and walnut, chocolate with red glacé cherries, and fruitcakes so packed with currants previously soaked in tea that they tasted mineral. As well as this there were Victoria sponges with either strawberry or raspberry jam and thick butter icing between each layers. A slice of one of these cakes was served with a cup of strong, earth-brown tea, presented in an apple-green or an aubergine cup and saucer and poured from a large, chipped, cream, enamelled teapot. Books with forbidding olive or ochre fabric covers, all with their dust jackets missing, were lined up on the trestle tables next to the tea stand, which was next to tables of broken toys and bric-a-brac – white china figurines of rabbits, shepherdesses, carthorses and small glass shoes and kittens and puppies; figures of Welsh women in traditional costume with black conical hats; small metal models of Spitfires, Hurricanes, Lancasters, Flying Fortresses and Mosquitos, with their camouflage green for land or occasionally taupe for sea, the dull grey of the die-cast lead alloy showing where the paint had been worn away or chipped by the previous owner; and lines of Dinky cars, pickup trucks, lorries and buses. There were tins of marbles, old military medals resting on small fabric cushions with their ribbons, portraits and books on Winston Churchill and the Queen, the Battle of Britain and Dunkirk.

The hall was permanently full of dust. It could be seen thickening the air, circling and floating around us in eddies, clearly visible by the light that poured in from the skylights above us and so dense that it seemed unlikely that anyone could breathe properly, that everyone's lungs were impeded. The dust came from everywhere, from the piles of dark flannel trousers, often still with their striped braces attached by buttons to the inside, from women's floral dresses with their belts and belt loops in the same matching fabric, from girdles, crocheted cardigans, knitted woollen tea-cosies, the trench coats and three-piece suits of the recently deceased, all with their waistbands yellowed with age.

Jumble sales started at two-fifteen in the afternoon. I would arrive early and queue on the recently disinfected wooden floor. There would be jostling and pushing against the locked doors before they opened. When they were finally unlatched, we spilled into the hall as though popped from a cork, racing for the bric-a-brac stall where the glass ornaments, the puppies and kittens, the model cars and aeroplanes waited patiently for their new owners. Sometimes Simon would come too, picking up as many of the toy aeroplanes as he could, his bony hands scouring books for the history of flight, his skin blue-tinged, his coughing continual, his skeleton apparent through his clothes.

Once when I was older and I could finally speak again I helped out at a jumble sale, and there I served Mr Bubyage over the wooden trestle tables where it was my pleasure to let him have everything he wanted for the tiniest sum of money. There was a glimmer of recognition of our annual shared seconds together, the path he made and the cold jars of honey he gave us sometime before Christmas. His eyes, which seemed to sink deeper into his face as he aged, smiled at me at this corruption; the teenager holding the goods he wanted, determining the price of the things he needed. But he magnanimously held out his hand, contradicting the law of nature, the usual law of order that means adults hold sway over children, and purchased from me a dark suit with braces, some shirts without collars and a tin of shortbread with a picture of a coracle floating on the water on its lid. And as he handed over the money he spoke to me again in a language I could not understand, the utterances guttural and formed, it seemed, at the back of his throat, his tone insistent, his body leaning towards mine in what I realised, as he handed over the money to me, was the manner of a conspiracy.

One day, when Simon was eighteen, he decided to follow a macrobiotic diet. As this was the early 1980s none of us had heard of macrobiotics but Simon had acquired a book with a seaweed-green cover, *Basic Macrobiotics*, written by Herman Aihara. It stated:

> Suffering incurable diseases at the age of 18, George Ohsawa learned about the macrobiotic diet. Using these principles he restored his own health.

Simon changed his diet to brown rice, seaweed, miso, daikon, grated ginger and vegetables. Dairy food, sugar and eggs became his enemies, ice-cream the food eaten in the first circle of hell, meat the devil incarnate. He cooked his own meals using a bamboo steamer, refusing to eat what we ate and continually reminding us that,

> George Ohsawa cured himself. His kidneys were failing. He had eczema. He had terrible breathing difficulties. The same as me.

Simon also refused to take antibiotics. When his big toe became infected after he cut it on the pedal of his bicycle, we watched it gradually turn red, then maroon, then a glistening black. His solution to this was to carve a hole in a fresh onion and place his toe in it. This, he told me, would 'draw' the infection, the onion juice acting as an antiseptic. For weeks Simon went to bed with a fresh onion Sellotaped to his foot. His toe became worse and worse until it was a grotesque version of a toe, a Théâtre du Grand Guignol toe, a Hammer Horror prop of an infected toe.

My father pronounced grave warnings: 'You could lose that toe of yours'; or, 'That toe might have to be amputated if it develops gangrene'; and even, 'People die of septicaemia.' My brother's answer was always the same:

> My immune system is ruined. All those antibiotics and other drugs I was given when I was a child destroyed it. The only way to strengthen my immune system is to rebuild it so that it can deal with infections itself. That's why I'm using the onion.

Eventually Simon's toe healed, though the rest of him became excruciatingly frail. I could see his body tormenting him, the dark circles around his eyes spreading across his face, his ribs visible under his shirt, his hip bones showing under his constantly slipping-down trousers. At dinner Simon would do verbal battle with my father.

> After the bomb fell on Hiroshima, people who had eaten miso soup survived.
> *What bloody drivel.*
> Their gut microbes offered them protection against the effects of the radiation.
> *You-talk-utter-nonsense – dangerous tripe.*

A silence would ensue, which would eventually be broken by Simon launching into another fact.

Have you noticed that Princess Di's eyes are unusual?
You can see a white sliver of her eyeball underneath her
pupil and above her lower eyelid?
Her sclera?
Sanpaku.
What are you talking about, sanpaku?
Princess Di's eyes tell you she's got a condition called
sanpaku. She's out of touch with herself.
Out of touch with herself?
Kennedy had sanpaku too.
You talk highly irritating nonsense. You're meant to be educated.
What-schools-and-universities-are-turning-out-these-days-is-
nothing-short-of-socially-catastrophic.

A silence would then follow before my father ostentatiously
added salt to his food and asked my brother if he would like
some beef dripping.

Would you like some beef dripping? I'm going to have some.
Beef dripping?
A bit of fat is good for you.
Do you know how poisonous beef dripping is? You
have to balance yin and yang.
Ying and who?

And so it went on – diet as emotional warfare, food as ammu-
nition, the battleground the kitchen table.
 Beef dripping, together with raw mince, raw eggs and raw

192

onion, was my father's favourite food. A constant supply was kept in the fridge. He would spread thick layers on brown toast and add lots of salt. Often he would follow this with a steak tartare, mixing the raw minced meat, raw eggs, raw onion and pepper in a white bowl with a fork. As steak tartare and dripping were effectively the opposite of a macrobiotic diet, the consequence was that, at mealtimes, Simon and Hans, who ate their respective foods together, one with meat and no grain, the other with grain and no meat, would incessantly argue. Simon would also periodically make announcements.

I'm getting a microlight.

And where will you keep that?

In your garage.

You're not keeping a microlight in my bloody garage.

I've ordered it.

You've ordered it?

I've placed a deposit.

Well, you're not keeping it in my garage. I won't allow it.

There's no room.

It won't be there for long.

Absolutely not.

But despite my father's protests, my brother kept his microlight in my parents' garage for years. He even arranged to take off and land in a field not far from their house. It turned out he could handle his microlight well and would return from his trips into the sky elated by the purity of the air.

'Up there is the only place I can breathe in.' He would take us up in his black XL-R-flex-wing-with-Rotax-engine, one at a time, coaxing us to sit behind him, each of us clinging to the metal frame of the trike, or holding his waist. The tiny engine revved like a lawnmower on full power, and the microlight gave a disconcerting bounce across the field, which he had previously checked for molehills and flattened with a spade. We'd race past the nearby barbed-wire fences, grass near our hands, in a parody of international commercial flight with its tarmac runways and control towers. Then we would lift away, slowly tipping towards the sky, a gradual climb, Simon pushing the A-frame away from his chest, wrestling with it in the air's strange and blustering currents, then up further towards the clouds, then through them, surrounded by them, their texture a surprise, slight dampness, cold on the skin, hands holding onto the trike, knuckles sticking out, looking around at the cloud's interior, the colour of an X-ray's white parts, sticking my tongue out, tasting the cloud in my mouth (so this is what it tastes like), until we're above them, the sun a sphere on the horizon, bright lighted, the moon partially out, pale, hard to discern against the sun's rays bouncing off the top of the clouds. There we would fly around in circles before descending back through the clouds, then flying together over our childhoods, the hospital, Pentrosfa, the hills, the lake, the schools, the park, the houses we lived in, Castle Hill, all of it flattened out from the air, a panopticon of memories.

Then he would pull the A-frame towards his chest, tipping

the nose of the microlight towards the ground. I would watch the ground come towards us, until the last moment when Simon would quickly raise the microlight's nose by pushing the A-frame away from him again, landing on the wheelbarrow tyres, bouncing across the field, past the flattened molehills, just like the magazines said you could, the engine screaming in our ears. Then climbing out, me relieved to be back on the ground, my brother elated, bossy, demanding, adrenaline surging, a six-foot-two, walking, black-eyed skeleton, his spirits soaring, a trace of him left behind in the clouds where he longed to return. 'Anybody else want a go?' My father now, strapped behind him, trundling over the field, then disappearing into the air and through the clouds too before returning, bump-bump, coming to rest by a hedge. Then my brother dismantling his machine, piece by piece, bulldog clips and stainless-steel wires, and storing it again in our parents' garage. And my mother beside herself with a mixture of pleasure and fear at the force of the child she'd saved all those years ago with oxygen and her care and her compliance with his demands that arrived from him down the string telephone.

Later Simon took my father on a microlight rally around Britain. Then he went further, flying from Spain to the UK, over the Pyrenees with maps, before GPS, landing in fields near petrol stations to fill up with fuel so that he could carry on flying, using an air bed as safety equipment in case his engine failed while he crossed the Channel, carrying a tent to sleep in where the second passenger would normally sit. At night he parked in fields. As he told me later,

Flying over the Pyrenees was the most difficult thing. I had to find the point where they were at their lowest and then fly through the gap between the highest peaks. Even though it was summer, there was still snow and scree next to me as it's over 10,000ft high. Finding the route as the light was failing and my hands were freezing took a bit of concentration. You have to hug the downwind side of the valleys as you're approaching the summit.

And then he was healed. The diet over the years had appeared to work. It had taken him a decade of rigorous adherence to macrobiotics. George Ohsawa's writings had allowed him to cure himself. 'My immune system is strong now.'

He learned to pilot a helicopter, a Robinson R22, the smallest, most delicate helicopter there is, its Plexiglas-fronted canopy and tiny controls possessing a minimalist beauty. He would take me for flights in one that he had hired. The sensation of leaving the ground vertically then hovering at tree height, before rapidly being lifted up vertically thousands of feet into the air at 1,200ft a minute was thrilling. It was as though we were being pulled towards a secret source in the heavens. I would watch the ground fall away from my feet, receding quickly, seeing it in its entirety through the R22's Plexiglas bubble. It was the closest thing to angelic flight I have experienced, with its hovering and its climbing vertically through the air. Helicopters reveal the collective imprint of angels' flight in all their designers' minds. 'I don't take risks,'

Simon tells me, his face a copy of my father's; clenched teeth, firm mouth, jutting chin:

> 'The margin for error on an R22 is too low to take any
> risks. The blades have very low inertia so that if they
> slow below 80 per cent of their maximum speed they
> stall and so the helicopter crashes.'
> What happens if the engine fails?
> 'There are one point six seconds before the pilot has to
> activate the emergency procedures.'
> And if you don't manage to do this within that
> time period?
> 'A delay of more than one point six seconds is fatal.'

My brother laughs as he tells me this, his eyes are cheerful and his even, white-toothed smile spreads wide across his face.

4.7

In the morning we rise early to visit my father's father's grave in the Weißensee cemetery. My father has had a restless night and has woken me during it, tapping my shoulder, frightened, wanting to know where he is, his eyes dark canisters, his shoulders hunched high, his right arm outstretched towards me half asleep, not quite aware. Eventually he calms, returns to his bed and sleeps. Throughout the night I'm woken by him calling and shouting, sounds rather than words, fearful noises, dark shards. When he emerges into the thin light of morning he is calm and, although pallid, alert, and insists on wet shaving before we leave for the graveyard, something that he has done every morning for his entire life. It's something he recommends to everyone: 'It's an excellent way to start the day.' But shaving, despite his years of practice, is something he's never fully mastered, partly because he insists on using a very heavy old-fashioned razor and partly because he simply chops at his face as quickly as he can. The consequence of these two factors is that he often cuts himself. His way of managing the blood that bleeds out of these incisions is to place small pieces of toilet paper on them to aid coagulation, though often this isn't successful, and so although some of the toilet-paper-mixed-with-blood stays on his face and begins, as it dries, to form a scab, other pieces fall to the floor and so form behind him a short trail of blood-sodden tissue. Where the toilet paper has fallen off his face his cuts continue to bleed, small drips occasionally leaking from him onto the ground. The combination of the toilet paper stuck to his face, the dried blood and the openly bleeding cuts is something that we, his family, have become used to over the years but it's not a common look, either in the wider world or, on this particular morning, within the Grimm's Hotel.

We go down together in the stainless-steel lift to the hotel's foyer and sit at one of its smoked-glass tables. The lime-green chairs with chrome fittings are becoming familiar now. I fetch a cup of black coffee from a machine, as well as a plate of cooked meats, tomato, cheese and egg from a counter at the back of the hotel's foyer, which acts as a breakfast bar in the mornings. When I place the food in front of my father he gently leans his body forward until his head is several inches above it, and from this distance he eats, immediately, hurriedly, with determined focus, his eyes attentive to the shapes and textures of the food, his hands tremulous, his fingers gripping the knife and fork so tightly the veins on his large knuckles turn cobalt blue. From the time when he begins his food to the time when he finishes it he is uncommunicative, unavailable to anyone, the physical act of eating seeming itself to consume him. He eats without stopping, one mouthful following on immediately from the next, a forkful of food arriving at his lips while the previous mouthful is being swallowed, his mouth perpetually full, his jaw working, his teeth grinding continuously, transforming food into a life-giving paste.

He divides the plate invisibly into a number of narrow strips, finishing each one completely before moving on to the next. The process looks like a small-scale, co-ordinated land clearance. He moves resolutely, strip by strip, from the left-hand side of his plate to the right as though enacting an ancient ritual, and he remains, while illuminated by the sharp light of the halogen downlighters that are fixed into the hotel's ceiling, and while his brown polished shoes rest upon one of the hotel's tangerine carpets, isolated.

When he finishes his food he polishes his plate with bread, as he has always done, and then slowly sits back upright and returns his mind to the inhabited world. He sits imperiously on the end of his chair and from this position begins to pass judgement on the other guests who have recently arrived and who are starting to eat their breakfasts.

Just look at that pile *of food she's eating.*

Not so loud, Dad.

Well, really.

It's breakfast. At a hotel. It's what people do.

No wonder she's carrying so much visceral fat.

Please, Dad. Be quiet.

So much adipose tissue. Look at it.

Hans.

It's awful.

It's not awful.

And dangerous.

Why's it dangerous?

It stresses her heart, her liver, her kidneys, her spleen, her adrenal glands. That's why it's dangerous.

I glance at the woman he is talking about who is, as far as I can see, of normal build and weight, and I smile at her hoping to ameliorate any offence my father might have given. I assume that she might have heard him as the table she is sitting at is unnervingly close to ours. It's a strategy I've used since childhood, one I am not proud of and even ashamed of – a different part of me wants my father to have to deal with the reaction that he engenders so that I do not have to field people's hostile looks. The smile I give to members of the public my father has offended is one that comes easily to me as I have practised it regularly since childhood. It's one that is excruciating, embarrassing, that hurts my face as I do it and, as a friend of mine points out, is the sweet, sad smile of a little shit.

Do you know how much obesity costs the NHS each year?

And he's off on his usual rant against people who carry any excess weight at all. It's a crime for him, one he is unable to forgive easily, one that is dragging down civilisation as well as his beloved NHS.

Have you ever run a marathon?

No.

Why not?

Never wanted to.

Keeps fat off. I did them at your age.

I know you did.

Did twenty-two. Or twenty-three. Or twenty-four.

I remember.

Didn't stop running until I was eighty-two.

Your house is plastered with pictures of you running.

Your sister does them.

I know she does.

She's fast.

I know she is.

Whereas you're putting on weight.

I jog. Occasionally.

Jog? Occasionally? Well you're not jogging hard enough.

I stop answering. The bickering peters out and we sit in silence. It's a familiar, loaded, unbearable silence, this moment between us, and I am reminded yet again why I have to keep away from him. He drives intimacy away with his perpetual undermining criticism. The trauma he endured as a child has seeped into him and it cannot be removed by me, even momentarily, no matter how much I try. I wonder if he feels close to anyone as he sits in front of me with small trickles of blood on his face. Something was stolen from him on that train journey and it cannot come back. Those who survive such things as he has survived have survived the death of their previous life and yet are forced to live on in the world while holding this death inside them. It falls upon them to live their lives from the point of view that extends beyond their first death. As Sebald tells us, they must live beyond 'their own partial extinction'. Survivors such as my father can only be understood from the 'complex insight that ... those who survive collective catastrophes have already experienced their death'.[1]

Sebald's perception has led me to consider how new life might emerge after its own death and to the conclusion that it must give birth to itself. My father, in an act of supreme will, reconstructed himself while at the same time holding his own 'partial extinction' inside himself. He parented himself, reconstituted himself and so lived on. It is why he does not look back, or recall, or engage with his past, why he never regales us with his childhood stories or talks about anything German. 'The outcast,' Sebald goes on to tell us, while referring to Hans Erich Nossack's writing, 'dared not look back, since there was nothing behind but fire.'[2]

We finish breakfast. I ask the man at reception how to get to the Weißensee Jewish cemetery. He locates it on one of the hotel's maps and then, with a flourish, does his roll-of-maps trick, landing a fresh map like a magic carpet in front of us. 'And does the hotel rent out bicycles?' says my father. 'Yes we do,' says the man.

And so we hire two bicycles and head to the north-east of Berlin, my father leading the way, past Alexanderplatz, past the Fernsehturm, along wide streets with what he notes are 'excellent cycling lanes', past high housing and hairdresser's, past cafés, and shoe shops and those selling white goods. As the route is slightly uphill we occasionally stop to catch our breath and so look around on Greifswalder Straße, noticing its unusual concentration of barbershops. There we see how men waiting in the queue for their haircuts sit in postures of assertion, legs open, backs firm, their gazes direct, and how this contrasts with the postures of those whose hair is being cut by the barber. Their heads lean back on the headrests of black-and-chrome chairs, necks at a strained angle, each man vulnerable, a posture of acquiescence.

We pass health food shops, shops selling mopeds, and general stores, my father now exerting himself, his breath strained. We cycle along Gürtelstraße and Puccinistraße then Herbert-Baum-Straße and arrive at the entrance to the Weißensee cemetery.

The cemetery covers 100 acres and is the second largest Jewish cemetery in Europe. It holds over 115,000 graves. We walk through its entrance. We each place a black kippah on our heads taken from a box of kippot attached to the wall at the entrance. Next to the entrance there is a memorial to the memory of all Jews murdered in each of the Nazi exter-mination camps. My father reads the names of the camps out loud, slowly, his voice clear. 'Auschwitz-Birkenau-Belzec-Chelmno-Janowska-Majdanek-Sobibor-Treblinka.' There is a large black stone, which has carved on it, in gold lettering:

THE BERLIN SHADOW

GEDENKE EWIGER

WAS UNS GESCHEHEN

GEWIDMET DEM GEDÄCHTNIS

UNSERER ERMORDETEN

BRÜDER UND SCHWESTERN

1933–1945

UND DEN LEBENDEN

DIE DAS VERMÄCHTNIS

DER TOTEN ERFÜLLEN SOLLEN

I ask my father to translate. He pauses and concentrates.

> *Remember what happened to us.*
> *This is dedicated to our brothers and sisters*
> *Who were murdered.*
> *The living should fulfil*
> *What the dead cannot do.*

We go to the reception area and are given a map of the grave-yard by a tall burly Jewish man with a large beard.

> How are we going to find your father's grave?
> *He's in one of the Urnenfelds.*
> A field of urns?
> *Exactly.*

We look at the map. It has four Urnenfelds marked on it.

Do you know which one your father's in?

Could be any of them.

You don't know?

How should I know?

We'll have to visit them all, then.

Looks like it.

Let's start with number one.

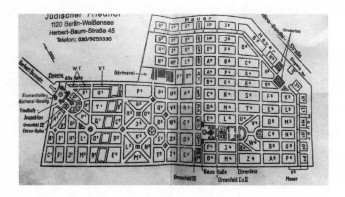

We start following the map to Urnenfeld I. We walk through the graveyard, which is empty of people and chock-a-block with the dead. It is full of thousands and thousands of graves that no one visits. There is no one left alive to do the visiting. The dead have been deserted by the murdered. Trees sprawl throughout, their thin trunks cluttering the ground, greedy for light, straggling on paths, growing from graves, poking out of walls, their roots interconnected under the ground, their falling leaves a disintegrating canopy. The trees' roots have pushed headstones to one side, cracking and breaking many of them. They have tilted huge red-and-black marble mausoleums, whose polished grandeur is chipped and faded, their leaning and natural decay a more eloquent memorial to their dead's remains than when bright and new and correctly angled. Most of the headstones are covered in ivy and weeds, many with missing letters, some in Hebrew, some in German, their absent letters giving their occupant surprising new names: '-ranke-stei-' and 'Ba-m' and 'Co—n' and 'L-wando-ski' and '–unki-' and 'Sh—ar' and 'הי-ש' and 'ל--ירבג'.

Leaves fall around us as we walk, like large melancholy confetti. They mottle the ground. We follow the map along narrow, cobbled paths, some smoothed and recently maintained, others covered with weeds that poke through at the edges and between each cobble. We walk for nearly twenty minutes, my father's face crumpling in the cold, his hood now protecting him as best it can, the cord used to tighten his hood flapping against his cheek.

With the aid of the map we walk through the cemetery until we find Urnenfeld I. It's an area with a hundred or so graves in it. I look at each of the names in turn. Some are clearly visible but most have been covered in moss, making any lettering difficult to read. My father is standing some distance from me, fidgeting, biting his fingers, remote, moving around, shifting from one leg to the other, wandering around, picking up leaves and moving them, kicking them gently with his feet. I am bent, my back doubled, my neck cricked at a funny angle, peering at names through the thick lenses of my glasses. At the head of one of the rows I find the grave of my father's father, my grandfather, Walter Lichtenstein. The sight catches me. Seeing his name in letters on a grave makes me suddenly transparent: my head spins, my limbs weaken. 'It's here,' I say. My father walks over and joins me, quietening at the sight of his father's grave, seemingly all of a sudden tranquil and even serene, his feet placed evenly apart on the ground, the weight of his body on the soles of his feet connected to the stabilising earth, his fidgeting stopped, his hands away from his mouth, his body still. He holds his arms behind him and bends his head to the ground. We stand in silence. I think of holding his hand or putting my arm through his but I don't. He wouldn't like it. Nor would I.

Walter Lichtenstein's gravestone is in the shape of an urn and covered in a thin layer of lichen that has turned a soft, citric green. The urn shape has been achieved by pouring concrete into a rubber mould. It's situated close to a tall

Scots pine, or *Königskiefer*. Its long, evergreen branches shelter the grave, so that the urn is still in good condition. Small pieces of fir litter the ground, some brown, some green. I pass my father two of the stones I've been carrying in my pocket.

I brought these from outside your house in Wales.

I place three small stones in a line upon Walter's grave. My father places his two larger stones next to them. We listen to the sounds of the trees moving. The air brushes our skin. 'There we are,' says my father, softly, and then, 'I hope it makes you feel better.' 'It does,' I say, 'it's a relief.' 'I'm glad about that,' he says, grace shining from him. I want to say out loud, 'How does it make you feel?' but it's too crass a question, too violent in its simplicity. It would require from him a verbal answer that is impossible to cohere. It would require a pinning down. And, anyway, it frightens me to think about what might happen if he began to answer this, for the answer could unravel my father's carefully constructed façade. His façade might fall away to reveal the thing that is within him, the thing that inhabits his intestines and his stomach, the thing that if it did emerge into the light would whimper at first and then destroy him, as well as those around him. It would do so immediately and without conscience. It is the terror that he carries inside himself. The most terrible thing. It must not be allowed out into the open air. He will not let it. We all know it's there. It's what I hear during his nightmares. It's what I see in his nails. It's what his eyes reveal. It must not be uncovered. He will not have it. Nor will I let him. His decision to take his own suffering all the way to his own grave, unspoken, is a devout act, a mitzvah.

'I suppose you're going to lie down now,' says my father. 'Yes,' I say, 'in a minute, if you don't mind. I'm sorry it's so odd.' 'You-do-what-you-bloody-like,' says my father, 'just don't ask me to join in and anyway you've-always-been-odd-very-bloody-strange-if-truth-be-known.' The insult does not sting; on the contrary, it makes me smile. He is holding it in, the thing. *He is sparing me.*

I lie down next to my grandfather's grave, quickly, without too much drama, though there is something here that presses me down, squeezes my chest, won't let me get back up. I have to fight to stand back up and then I have to lie down again. When I stand again, I am curiously wobbly and oddly connected with the ghosts that are swirling. 'God knows why you do this,' says my father. 'I can't quite work it out either,'

I say. 'Bloody-odd,' says my father, who then looks away. And so I put my arms around Walter Lichtenstein's urn and kiss it quickly, its rough surface prickling my lips, the lichen brushing my mouth, the concrete cold. It is the closest I can get to my grandfather and, although I know consciously that it is not close to him at all, it feels it to me, for the ground contains his mortal remains.

> You've never been here before?
> *I've told you that.*
> You didn't attend his funeral?
> *No.*
> Strange.
> *I fail to see why you're quite so fascinated. He was my father, not yours.*
> I know. But there's a gap. I can't get across it. It's caused me to . . .
> *Caused you to what?*
> . . .
> *What's the matter with you?*
> . . .
> *Spit it out.*
> . . .

But I can't spit it out. I cannot reply. My reply will not coagulate for it includes the words *not-wanting-to-be-alive-for-many-years* and *wanting-to-die* and *not-being-able-to-bear-life-even-though-it-is-the-most-beautiful-event-that-happens-to-me.* We stand for

longer in silence than we have ever stood together before.
He lifts his hand to his face. He turns his head towards me.

I want to go.

And so we leave. We walk back alongside the graves, through
the spinning leaves, over the rough paths that slope at their
edges, over weeds and under trees, tracing our route back to
the entrance with the aid of the graveyard's map.

We replace our kippot in the box on the wall, get back on
our bikes and set off. Because it's slightly downhill towards
the centre of Berlin we gain speed and so put our bikes into
their highest gear and head towards Alexanderplatz, now
pushing through the thickening air fast, our hands stiffening
with cold, making it harder to brake. We pass the barbers
and the coffee shops in something of a blur, the downhill
slope bestowing upon us vitality as well as speed, the release
from the graveyard a relief, an injection of life, my father
in front, a whizzing Holocaust survivor in his eighties, a
mixture of glee and grief in his furiously pedalling legs, me
a thrill of pride at his unlikely strength, his coat turned up,
his head towards the handlebars, beginning of all things to
streamline, letting the air pass over his back rather than hit
his body and slow him, crouching over the handlebars, chin
resting on them. He's racing me. O.M.G. We pass traffic,
cross junctions with trams on them, bump the wheels over
tram tracks, scoot past people entering or leaving their apartments; young couples with entwined hands, old people with

shopping trolleys, people struggling with their keys, people in cafés smoking outside. We sneak along pavements, past waiting cars, through lights about to turn red. We travel up a one-way street the wrong way, people calling at us as though we're daft.

When we reach Alexanderplatz we stop on the pedestrianised precinct and lean against our saddles. My father holds onto his bike and bends his head to the ground to catch his breath. 'I enjoyed that,' he rasps, his chest rising and falling quickly, the concrete paving stretching around us, the Fernsehturm now near us and above us. 'Something about pedalling bikes always cheers me up.' We are next to a café with a red fabric temporary roof that claims to 'mimic the shape of a Bedouin tent'. The fabric is covering its outdoor section and stretches across a series of hard wooden slatted benches that no one is using because it's far too cold to sit outside. It is as far away from a desert as it is possible to be. Neon lights lurk inside the surrounding shops, their light enfeebled behind large, flat, smooth, plate-glass windows.

We push our bikes west, my father almost freakishly fit for his age, his lean body muscular, his head tipped forward, his shoulders hunched up to his ears, his back bent, his chin jutting. 'Cycling reminds me of being a child,' he announces to no one in particular. We walk past an ornate carousel that spins slowly. No one is riding it at the moment. Its owner is wearing a jacket that has embroidered on its back 'Venetian Carousel, Horst Langenberg, Bertazzon, Italy'.

We move towards the fountain of Neptune at the far side of Alexanderplatz. 'This has been moved,' says my father. 'It used to be in the Stadtschloss gardens.' Now the fountain's background is comprised of the Marienkirche, the Fernsehturm and Berlin's red-brick town hall, the Rotes Rathaus. Water pours over Neptune. His trident leans on his shoulder. He is supported by centaurs with webbed feet who raise him into the air. Putti make mischief around him. Below him a turtle, a snake, a porpoise and a crocodile squirt water from their mouths. Statues of women sit at the base of the fountain, each in their own bronze world. We watch droplets arise as water cascades into the pool next to us. It causes a prismatic effect, small elusive rainbows.

I look over and I see my father. His eyes have turned a ferocious blue. They have retreated far back inside him. He stands motionless. His presence in this moment on Alexanderplatz is outside the order of things. It is taking place against the tide of history and I am reminded of what

I have always known: that he, and I too, will soon pass and die, that the fountain and all its surroundings, the buildings and all the roads, the Fernsehturm and the paving stones will disappear as they are bound to, and that to belong to the particular intensity of this moment, to be within its existence as it drapes its kindness over us both, is a triumph, a privilege. And must be enough.

4.8

My sister Jane rang to tell me. Afterwards I lay face down on my kitchen floor. I felt a huge weight press me into the ground. I rang my parents to tell them. I told my father first. I asked him to pass the phone to my mother. I told her and that's when I heard her scream again.

Simon was flying with his friend Martin. They were both very experienced pilots. They were flying a Robinson 22 from Italy to the UK. They crashed a few kilometres north-west of Nice, very near Tourrettes-sur-Loup. The air investigation report concluded that a gust of wind had tipped the helicopter to one side and Martin, who was piloting at the time, had overcorrected, leaning the helicopter too far the other way so that one of its blades clipped the left-hand side of the cabin as well as one of the toes of the helicopter's landing skids. The sheared-off tip of the blade was found weeks later, 400 metres from the crash site. Damage to an engine is possible to deal with, but damage to one of the blades means the helicopter loses more than 80 per cent of its lift and falls from the sky, the pilot and passenger waiting for their deaths as it does so. The helicopter came down over steep woods in a valley on a bright winter's day. Both Simon and Martin were pushed through the Plexiglas canopy and died immediately, their bodies broken into pieces. At the time all any of us could do was try to survive from one moment to the next, for grief shrinks the future, makes it contract, makes it disappear.

The conclusion in the air accident report was that they should never have been flying in such conditions. As Richard Mornington-Sanford wrote in helicopter magazine *Rotor Torque*, in an article entitled 'Why Martin and Simon Died',

> As with most accidents, this particular accident could have been prevented on the ground prior to take-off, as it was a poor decision to depart: therefore, the cause of the accident must be centred upon 'human factors'. In particular it involves something we call 'get-home-itis' (referred to in the French accident report as 'target destination'), which is the leading cause of helicopter accidents.

My parents were beside themselves with sorrow, their etched faces hollow, their bodies bent double. Simon had lived near them, saw them most and was closest to them. It was during this time that I began to understand grief, for grief was a thing that arrived inside me. It took up residence. It had a physical presence. Grief invaded me and would not let me go. It eroded my body, making my hips stiff and my fingers arthritic. For a time it took away joy and replaced it with sticky mud. It is, as all will tell who have lost, something that alters the world completely. It is exhausting, a pummelling, a racing of the heart, a cascade of the mind.

I visited my parents as soon as I could and stopped off at

my brother's house. There I took off my shoes and put on his; a pair of brown polished brogues. I got into his old bottle-green Audi estate and drove. When I first sat in the car the leather seat was far back, the steering wheel low, just as he had left them. I pulled the seat forward, changing from his driving position to mine. And then I set off through the Welsh Marches into the hills of Wales.

4.9

We leave Alexanderplatz and push our bikes along Spandauer Straße. We pass the Berlin Dungeon, '*mit kombitickets bis zu 50% sparen*', the Apotheke Hackesches Quartier, the Brotmeisterei steinecke, past MUJI and Moleskine and IQOS, until we stand outside a café with wooden doors and a large picture window, the Hackescher Hof.

The Hackescher Hof looks as though it hasn't changed since it was opened in 1906. Its walls have panelled wood, its ceiling is smoothly plastered, its cornices are elegantly aligned. A large number of small lights have been set into the ceiling, installed in a geometric pattern.

Its chairs are wooden and its square tables have single columns with square bases instead of legs. One of the walls is covered in a selection of black-and-white photographs. These show, on its lower part, the café soon after it opened in 1906, full of customers reading newspapers, eating and drinking coffee, relaxing in wooden chairs. The photographs hung on the middle part of the wall show what happened to the Hackescher Hof during the Second World War, when it lay derelict and gutted, then during the 1950s when it was used as a store, during the 1960s when it was used as a garage and car park full of Trabants, and during the 1970s when it was boarded up and dilapidated. The photographs placed higher up on the wall show the café being restored throughout the 1990s and situated at its top are pictures of the present day, customers relaxing again with coffees and cakes. A hundred years of history on a wall.

> *It's more or less as I remember it.*
> You came here as a child?
> *I did.*
> You liked cafés?
> *As did my father, my mother, my uncles, my grandparents.*

We take a seat by the window that overlooks the street. A waiter arrives. My father orders scrambled eggs with smoked trout and smoked salmon, dark rye bread and *ein Kaffee schwarz*. The waiter, while holding his pencil in the air, turns to me,

> I'll have the same please.

I thought you were a vegetarian.

Occasionally I eat fish.

So you're not.

I am mainly.

Either you are or you're not.

You know, I've always wondered.

What?

What he was like.

Who?

Your grandfather. My great-grandfather.

It's a long time ago.

Was he orthodox?

Reform.

I look at my father. He is sitting comfortably. His body is beginning to settle into the café after the cold of the graveyard.

Where did he die?

In our flat.

How?

Hanged himself.

Where?

From the window frame in the bathroom.

Who found him?

My grandmother.

Where were you?

With friends.

What happened?

My grandfather was beaten up in his own house in Rotenburg an der Fulda. That evening he left his home and came to live with us in Berlin. He came together with my grandmother.

My father suddenly hesitates — a fractional pip of silence, a negligible tear in the fabric. His voice lowers. He looks down at the tabletop.

After he arrived he stopped talking to anyone.
. . .
Except for me.
. . .
Then I stopped talking to him.

He places the nails of his left hand to his mouth.

My mother continually asked me to go into his room.

He begins to bite the nail of his middle finger.

Didn't want to.

Bites the nail of his index finger.

Went on for some time.

Small bites of the nail of his ring finger.

Didn't leave his room.

Eyes glazed.

And then.

Eyes down.

Felt guilty about it ever since.

I look at him.

Very guilty.

. . .

If you must know.

You shouldn't feel guilty.

I'll feel what I like.

But you were a child. There's nothing to be guilty about. Guilt is a useless emotion. You shouldn't feel guilty.

My father raises his eyes. He takes his hand away from his mouth. He looks at me with one of his looks. His eyes reach back into the depths of his body before sending their penetrating beam out towards me.

The trouble with you is . . .

What's the trouble with me?

The trouble with you is . . .

What?

You're a pious little shit.

His insult stings. And it makes the Hackescher Hof become, all of a sudden, vividly alive. My great-grandfather is here. He is lying next to the window frame. He wears his noose. He wears an Iron Cross, second class. Walter arrives. He stands next to my chair. The furniture I am sitting on is warming up. Heat is coming off the chairs and tables. The air is rising from their surfaces. It's burning me. All the dead I know are swirling around me. I am flicked out of myself and look down upon myself. And I see them. All the people who have ever been seated in this café, the secret lovers, the business dealers, the families with their children, the hipsters, the fascists, the communists, the Stasi informers, Bertolt Brecht and Helene Weigel with Walter Benjamin and Caspar Neher, hunched over rye bread and fish discussing the *Verfremdungseffekt*, people eating their breakfasts with silver pots of coffee, people picking at tiny cakes in the afternoon, people at huge sprawling lunches with cigars, eating dinner *mit Fleisch* and oysters on trays with their sea-silver shells stacked to heights that touch the cornices. They teem into the room, with their furs and their police uniforms, their swastikas, their East German suits, their tattoos and pierced lips, their kippot, their wigs. They are a mixture of Goya's *The Third of May 1808* combined with versions of the woman in Paula Rego's *The Policeman's Daughter*. I climb down from the ceiling. My body vibrates.

Suicide.

What about it?

Is it carried in the genes?

In the genes?

Do you think suicide is carried in the genes?

No.

For years I couldn't sleep, thinking I was bound to do it. That it was in my genes. That I was obligated.

Suicide?

Yes.

Obligated? What are you talking about?

Suicide skips a generation. So it's landed on my shoulders. And because I'm the oldest son it was inevitable I'd have to do it. And I have the same middle name as Walter.

It's got nothing to do with genes or names.

I'm not so sure.

My grandfather was beaten and pushed out of his home. He served in the German infantry during the First World War. I've told you before, he was awarded an Iron Cross, second class. My father's businesses were smashed. His neighbours ignored him. People refused to serve him in shops. It's got nothing to do with genes.

The plates of scrambled eggs and smoked fishes arrive. A small white pot containing horseradish rests upon each one. Two slices of cucumber and two of lemon have been placed at the plates' edges. The whole meal has been sprinkled with slivers of green spring onions. As I eat, I feel the pungent horseradish make its way up the back of my throat and into my nose. The irritation is welcome. It connects me back to my body. I taste the combination of both smoked fishes, feel the density of the dark seeded bread under my fingers. I see the pattern of one of the slices of lemon on the edge of the plate. My chest tightens up. My neck tenses. My stomach contracts. We're having the conversation we've needed to have our whole lives. We have been unable to do so up to now. The thoughts we have harboured inside ourselves have been too difficult to bring to the surface. Our bodies would not allow our thoughts to be thought. The end of our thoughts could not be borne. I say,

Did you settle in Wales to get away from all this?
Yes.
And did you go to shul when you were a child?
Until my father committed suicide. Then never again.
Pesach and Chanukah and Yom Kippur? Did you observe them?
When my father was alive.
And so you answered the four questions at Passover because you were the youngest male in the house?
The Mah Nishtanah?
Yes.
I answered the Mah Nishtanah.

My father looks at me again. I take one of the slices of lemon off my plate and place it on the corner of the table we're sitting at. I count its eleven segments. I notice the way the colour of the peel gradually changes from yellow at its edges to white as it progresses towards the centre and how its peel softens to become its pith. I notice that two of its pips have been sliced into two by a sharp knife. I notice the way the lemon pulp shines and how this contrasts with the black of the tabletop and its wooden edging. I take out my phone and take a picture of it.

For-God's-sake-will-you-stop-playing-with-your-bloody-food-it's-meant-to-be-eaten-you're-not-a-bloody-child-it's-like-being-with-a-10-year-old-and-that-bloody-phone-of-yours-is-going-to-drive-me-to-the-point-of-utter-insanity.

I look up from the glowing lemon slice and I see in front of me a man so courageous it takes my breath away. It is almost unbearable to talk about what he has lived through let alone has to live with. My brother's death has given me the small-est taste of how paralysing grief is. I look down at the floor and at the small metal hexagonal kick plates that have been screwed onto the base of the tables. What do I know about anything? He has looked into the abyss, leapt and jumped high enough to find the land on the other side.

> *My whole life I've had to watch you waste yours away. If I'd*
> *had your start in life . . .*
> I didn't know any other Jews.
> *You knew Mr Bubyage.*
> Was he a Jew?
> *Why do you think he brought round honey at Chanukah?*
> *Why do you think he continually muttered Yiddish to us?*

The café is nearly empty, though for me now migrainously starting to fill up again with imagined historical populations scrutinising copies of *Die Nürnberger Gesetze*. Now Mr Bubyage has arrived with his pinprick eyes, peering at his own copy while pushing his bike and covered in his bloody concrete dust. He is sitting across from me, tipping his hat to the mute waiter. I wish it didn't do this, my brain, on overflow, gushing volumes of images of the murdered and the dead, uncontrollable, their banter and their chatting addictive, their hopes infectious, their clothes seductive, their dark eyes full of love, flirting on the chairs and under the tables in their lace and wool. They're behaving most unsuitably for the gravity of the situation. Their chests are heaving.

The waiter arrives. He has been sitting on a chair in the corner. I assume that he's been listening to us because every time I catch his eye he looks like he's fixed his gaze upon our table. Unless he's just an excellent, though silent, waiter. We order more coffee.

Your mother? She survived. How?

She'd heard that a group of lawyers were specialising in a particular pretence in order to help Jews declassify as Jews.

What was the pretence?

My mother's mother Wyla had to testify in court that she'd had an affair with another man who was a Christian, so proving that Ruth was illegitimate and so a racial mixture, a Mischling.

Is that what happened?

My grandmother pretended that she had had an affair with a Christian doctor and so claimed that my mother was the doctor's child, the result of the affair.

She testified?

Yes.

And the doctor?

He testified too.

A Christian German?

Yes.

What was his name?

I don't know. He saved my mother's life.

We should find out. He must have been a brave man.

You're right.

But wasn't your grandmother Jewish?

She had converted to Judaism to marry my grandfather.

So a lie saved them?

It was widely done in Germany. My mother was one of over one hundred thousand Jews saved like this. She was able to take off her Yellow Star in court.

The Nazis' *Mischling* laws saved your mother?

The Mischling *laws saved my mother.*

Coffee arrives on a circular tray with a heavy silver pot of hot milk. I stir it into my cup and lift it to my mouth, the familiar bitterness a stabilising kindness. Silence arrives between us. The story has unfolded in the Hackescher Hof.

A woman comes and sits at the table next to us. She reads a fashion magazine with intense concentration, as though it is a work of the most difficult philosophy. She leans towards the pages in a state of bliss, turning each page joyously. She is dressed in flowing black trousers, a silk black top and a black appliqué embroidered coat. She has long grey hair and wears heavy silver rings on all her fingers. A large grey scarf falls over her shoulders. Her partner arrives, a super-fit man, dressed from head to toe in black Lycra cycling gear, wearing a metallic red crash helmet that is tightly strapped underneath his chin, his feet clanking on the floor due to his cleated cycling shoes that turn his feet up at a curious angle, his legs shining due to excessive Lycra-isation. The woman looks up from her magazine and asks the man to order her a caffè latte and so he sets off back along the Hackescher Hof's parquet flooring towards the coffee bar, this sleek man with minimal body fat who is technically equipped to ride the Tour de France.

Just so you know, my story is a non-story. On the scale of other families' suffering it is nothing. I was lucky. So was she. As a family we were very, very lucky.

I know.

Cousins, second cousins to Auschwitz-Birkenau and Theresienstadt. My grandfather and my father to suicide. But Toni escaped. My mother lived.

The cycling man returns carrying two caffè lattes in tall glass cups on a small silver tray. His walk is an act of balancing finesse as his cycling shoes alter his posture so that he has to lean slightly backwards as he walks forwards. It is as though he is miming walking through a powerful and particularly consistent wind that is silently blowing through the café, but only at him. Impressively, while leaning back he keeps his tray horizontal, the white top of the lattes remaining perfectly aligned in their glasses. Perhaps he trained at Ecole Jacques Lecoq.

I suppose you're going to write all this down?

I will later.

My mother's uncle worked at Friedrichshain hospital. A surgeon. Moritz.

Really?

Very good friends with Einstein. Used to play with him in a string quartet. Sailed together on the Wannsee. When he died Einstein wrote his obituary.

My father brings his coffee cup to his lips.

You didn't know that, did you?

Of course I didn't know that.

I had a friend, Heinz Peter, who I liked very much.

And?

Escaped to France.

And?

Auschwitz.

When did you eventually come back to Berlin?

In 1950.

You met your mother then?

*She was living in the East. She was a communist so wanted to
live there and of course she wanted me to return to Germany.
But I told her then that I was now British.*

That must have been difficult.

Not for me.

But for her?

What do you think?

And then?

And then I returned to Britain.

When did you next see her?

Nineteen fifty-seven.

So after you left on the *Kindertransport* you only saw her
once between 1939 and 1957.

Yes.

Once in eighteen years.

My father calls our waiter over again and asks for the menu. He chooses a pudding with speed: '*Ein Crème Brûlée mit Passionfrucht und Belgischer Schokolade.*' We eat them quickly ('delicious'). The subject under discussion has now been closed.

We leave the Hackescher Hof and because we are full and we have eaten smoked fish and crème brûlée and we have talked more than we have ever talked, we walk along the wide pavement pushing our bikes together along Oranienburger Straße, past the repaired remains of the Neue Synagoge with its delicate cream-and-red brickwork and its dramatic, recently restored gold and glass cupola ('not my father's synagogue'), turn left down Tucholskystraße, right along Schiffbauerdamm, passing Brecht's Berliner Ensemble on our right and then further along the banks of the Spree, over the bridge on Luisentsraße, where, still pushing our bikes, we turn right onto Hannah-Arendt-Straße until we reach the Memorial to the Murdered Jews of Europe.

Some young people are playing hide-and-seek among the memorial's grey concrete blocks as we park our bikes, but it doesn't bother my father. We walk past them into the monument. The blocks at the memorial's edges are low and untroubling, almost inviting, but as we walk further in towards the centre of the memorial's 2,711 blocks the ground falls away unexpectedly, gradually sinking into the cooler earth. The cobbles under our feet become uneven. The ground begins to undulate. Progress becomes wearying. The blocks become taller and seem to suddenly loom above us, cutting out the light as the ground they are standing on lowers and as we move further inside. It begins to become first difficult, then impossible to see back towards the outside world. The blocks are like dolmen and have been set in lines that initially seem straight but on closer examination turn out not to be so. They have been set unevenly from each other. Suddenly I cannot see out of this 5-acre site and it is there that I feel the weight descend upon me again and that I suddenly am on my own, separated from my father. In the distance I catch glimpses of people, occasional flickers of them, as they walk past gaps between each of the blocks in the distance. But then they are gone and not seen again. I become separated from the surrounding city and its noise. The monument has been built upon one of the main areas that the Third Reich used to operate from, Albert Speer's buildings, now demolished by the government of East Berlin. I lie down on the ground of their foundations. Here the weight is huge and presses me hard. I hear Jean Améry's words float towards me:

And suddenly I felt – *the first blow* – and knew – there is no 'banality of evil' and Hannah Arendt who wrote about it in her Eichmann book knew the enemy of mankind only from hearsay, saw him only through the glass cage ... When an event places the most extreme demands upon us, one ought not to speak of banality.[3]

Each visitor's route through the memorial is different. There is no definitive structure, though the outcome must be similar, an abrupt feeling of isolation and loneliness. I get back up and head towards the outer edges of the memorial and it is there that I see my father walking between the concrete blocks and it is then that I call him, and that is when he turns his head towards me and that is when I catch the following photograph of him.

4.10

Mr Marmalade was the name of our cat. My sister Jane had named him and he lived with us in Cae Hyfrydd on Pentrosfa. He was a slim and temperamental cat and I usually gave him a wide berth. Sometimes if I did stroke him he would wrap his front paws around my arm then scratch me with his back claws, scraping them painfully and drawing blood. We'd been given him by a farmer, which may account for why he was never particularly social and a fighter. Often he would lie in the front window peering out at the world, or recline on a chair. Sometimes he would whine for food but on the whole he was an unsympathetic cat as far as I was concerned. Once he disappeared for several days and we all became very worried. My mother made a small poster and put it on the front gate saying, 'Cat Lost', with a drawing and description of him.

Several days later Mr Marmalade appeared at the back door, extremely thin and tired, with one of his back legs missing. My father told us that Mr Marmalade must have been caught in an illegal 'gin trap', a fearsome device that grips an animal's leg and is impossible to get out of. That evening, while we ate supper, he went on to say that Mr Marmalade must have bitten his own leg off in order to survive, 'for the survival instinct is very strong'. The thought of Mr Marmalade eating his own leg sent shivers down all our spines and for years we debated, as children, whether we would be able to bite our own legs off if we too became caught in a gin trap or some other life-threatening situation. Mr Marmalade, despite being very weak, recovered, though naturally evolved a strange way of walking, using his front legs as a normal cat would and then hopping with his lone back leg, the stump of his other auto-cannibalised leg clearly visible. When it snowed you could see the idiosyncratic pattern of his prints on the ground, but he moved effectively and without apparent discomfort. Eventually Mr Marmalade left our home for our neighbour who fed him with cream and other fresh titbits, much to my sister's sadness, but not mine. There was something obdurate and unfriendly about Mr Marmalade and, despite my respect for the unimpeachable fortitude he had shown by eating his own leg, I was glad to see the back of him.

5.1

'I've been thinking,' says my father during breakfast. 'What's that?' I ask. He leans forward.

I want to take my father's last journey. I want to walk to our old apartment then take the journey to Bernau bei Berlin. That's where he took his own life. He hanged himself in a hotel there. Near Obersee bei Lanke.

We leave the Grimm's Hotel, walk again down Leipziger Straße until we reach the entrance to the Tiergarten. We step along its winding paths, pass its statues, the Englischer Garten then out of it next to the concrete blocks of flats, past Bellevue station, then over the bridge to my father's apartment. We stand by the front door. We touch its door handle. We gaze across the street, the Helgoländer Ufer. Beyond it is the River Spree. Above our heads is the bathroom where my father's grandfather Siegfried committed suicide. We cross the road, lean on the metal railings that run along the Spree's bank, gaze at the shrubs and trees on the opposite side of the river. To the right is a mixture of apartments and small hotels. Some are modern and built from steel and glass, others are older, clad in painted plaster. My father bites his nails, pushes his neck forwards, clenches his teeth, holds the railings with both hands.

We leave Helgoländer Ufer, walk back in silence across Moabiter Brücke, past the four statues of the bears, past the café that serves the Baumkuchen. A few cyclists pass us slowly, pedestrians carry bags strapped to their backs. Traffic is thin in this area of Mitte at this time of day. We reach Bellevue station. My father stops near its flower stall.

> *My father drove to work at his factory.*
> Whereabouts was it?
> *I don't know.*
> You had a car?
> *I want to take a taxi to Alexanderplatz.*

We stop a passing taxi. It drives us past the edge of the Tiergarten, past Goldelse, along the Straße des 17. Juni.

> *One morning I heard my mother and father screaming at each other. My father didn't come home after work. My mother rang the factory. They said my father had left soon after arriving. It became late. My mother rang the police. He must have parked at Alexanderplatz because that's where the police found the car the next day. Then he must have taken the train to Bernau bei Berlin. Then somehow got to Obersee bei Lanke.*

We arrive at Alexanderplatz, leave the taxi, enter the station and walk to Platform Eleven. We board the S–Bahn to Bernau bei Berlin. It travels underground for a while before emerging onto the surface in Berlin's outskirts. We pass through acres of engineering works. New tracks are being laid, new bridges are being built, roads are being redirected, buildings have been torn down. We pass rows of 1950s apartments with red-tiled roofs, and then, as we move towards the edges of the city, small allotments, most with wooden sheds and summer buildings, some with raised beds and neat grass, others wild and overgrown. We pass defunct brick-built railway buildings, old railway lines crowded with trees; we pass two large crumbling roundhouses that were used to turn around steam engines, for steam engines have only one direction of travel. We are in what was the East.

Of course this is not really my father's journey.

We change trains at Pankow. We walk through a subway to change platforms. On the next train we sit opposite an elderly couple who are about to go for a walk in the country, thick socks, leather boots. Another couple, young, with tattoos on their arms, are enchanting each other, white teeth glinting, giggles. Two teenage boys with long hair hold skateboards covered in stickers. This is an approximation of the last journey out of Berlin my grandfather, Walter, would have taken. For some reason it feels comforting. The air is clear. I feel at rest. My stomach is settled. I imagine that having decided what he was going to do, he would have been feeling calm. My friend Mark, who committed suicide when he was nineteen, seemed, retrospectively, particularly happy during the weeks before he took his own life. I can recall in vivid detail the exact moment he said goodbye to me for the last time, glancing a generous smile at me, dark, knowing eyes lit with ease as he waved to me outside the Grosvenor Stores, with its cast-iron columns painted cream at the Ridgebourne in Llandrindod. Perhaps some suicides can, to some extent, relax knowing that they don't have to struggle for much longer. The great quiet will come soon. Or perhaps not. Perhaps it is fearful terror all the way to the end.

The train comes to rest at the end of the line, Bernau bei Berlin. We leave the station and walk through the town to its park, the Stadtpark.

We used to come here together for picnics. We used to walk around this park. Toni and I.

The park is surrounded by medieval walls with two high towers. It has a small timber-framed gatehouse and well-kept gardens. My father remembers the way to it and around it, not that it's particularly complicated as it's fairly close to the station, but it's still a bit of a surprise since it's been over seventy years since he's been here.

We leave the park. Bernau bei Berlin is being restored, cobbled streets are being repaired, houses from the late 1800s that have fallen into disrepair are being repainted sombre colours, mustard, flax, sepia. Some of the buildings are dilapidated, paint flaking in long strips from their wooden window frames, their carved wooden doors graffitied. Bernau bei Berlin was part of the GDR. I use a toilet, the type that is placed on the pavement. It is made from stainless steel. I insert coins and the door slides open. It is spotless and smells of cleaning liquids. It has a stainless-steel toilet bowl and a stainless-steel back, which has a large swastika drawn on it in pencil. The door closes. I use soap and toilet paper to wash the swastika off, feeling slightly anxious not to mark the stainless steel, which is, I know from experience with my cooker at home, difficult to clean without leaving a smudge.

We walk back to the station then take a taxi to Lanke bei Bernau. The taxi is a large Mercedes painted, as all taxis here are, in cream, and it has black leather seats. The driver wears a plaid shirt of pillar-box red and powder blue with the word 'Texas' embroidered on the top of his left shoulder, visible over the back of his seat as he drives. The car's music system plays country and western, faintly, the regular beat of a banjo, the lyrics of love and loss, the longing for the American South filling the car.

After leaving the town we enter a forest. The tarmac covering the road is crumbling. The road's camber is so steep it inclines the car towards the ditch at the forest's edges so that we drive slowly through the broken light of the trees, across the road's breaking surface, at a tilt from the horizontal. The taxi driver tells us that Himmler used to use this road. *'Himmler fuhr oft diesen Weg'*; and as we don't answer he repeats this strange fact, *'Himmler fuhr oft diesen Weg.'* After twenty minutes the taxi emerges from the woods, passes through the small village of Lanke bei Bernau and draws into the Seeschloss Hotel's car park. My father shoots out of the taxi, walks quickly across the hotel's car park, up its steps to its front door. I catch up with him.

It hasn't changed much since I was last here.

We walk into the Seeschloss's reception. It's full of carved wooden furniture and has a wrought-iron banister next to a few steps that lead to a conservatory. I follow my father as he walks through the reception into the dining room. Its walls are sunflower yellow. Its ceiling is a brittle white and a number of brass lights with etched glass hang from it. There is a gold cornice. Heavy drapes, the colour of plum, have been placed above each window and a fitted carpet of cobalt blue has been stretched tightly to each of the room's corners. A thick, carved, dark wooden banister, set at waist height and running down the middle of the room, acts as a room divider. A few people are drinking coffee. A sign tells us: '*Das Seeschloss is seit uber 100 Jahren in Familienbesitz.*' Next to the sign there is a photograph of the hotel taken sometime during the early 1900s.

'We used to eat in this room,' says my father. We stand in it for a little while. My father walks to one of the windows, stands under the plum drapes and looks out at the lake opposite, the Obersee. A tall man in his early forties wearing a black waistcoat with a slightly grubby white unbuttoned shirt, unpolished shoes and ruffled blond hair approaches us and asks if we would like a coffee. 'Or a tea? A hot chocolate? Perhaps with a sandwich? Or a cake?' 'Not really,' replies my father as he continues to stare through the window.

We leave the hotel, walk down the steps outside its front door, cross the road opposite and walk to the northern edges of the Obersee. 'During the summer Father and I used to swim here together,' says my father. 'My mother sat on the banks and watched.' We walk for some time along the path at the lake's edge. It's sandy. It passes a children's playground that has, built within it, play equipment laid out in the approximate shape of a seventeenth-century galleon and at its edge a bin with a black plastic lid. We walk further. The path narrows. Plants and trees become crowded. My father stops and turns and gazes at the lake. Small ripples cross it. Roots of trees can be seen under the water's surface where the shore gives way to the lake. The trees opposite us on the far bank don't move because they're on the lee side and so sheltered from the wind. Their branches are quiet and darken the water that lies underneath them, turning it an opaque olive-green. Some branches hang so low they touch the water's surface. The water at the edge of the lake where we are now standing is unusually clear. I can see its bed of sand and stones. They look slightly larger than they really are due to the magnifying effect of water. We stand for some time.

There is no one around and so my father does what he occasionally does. He takes off his clothes and wades into the water naked. I watch him; the mixture of grey and dark hairs on his back, his pale skin, his strong shoulders, his long arms hanging by his sides, slightly inert, the water now up to his waist, his push as he leans forwards and begins to swim, the meniscus of the water glittering over him, his limbs crashing, his head submerged for a second before turning up for air. I take my clothes off too, though, unlike him, only down to my underpants, and follow him into the lake. Our clothes and passports and valuables are piled on the shore. The water's cold, and it hurts. I swim into the centre of the lake with my glasses on, a modest, unglamorous, breaststroke, my head above the water. I look towards the end of the lake. I see the Seeschloss. I look at it while swimming towards it, the shallow slope of its tiled roof, its new conservatory, the way tree branches hang at angles in front of it, its white brick and black timber walls. Walter swam here. I am in the frame of one of his last views, more-or-less-sort-of-not-quite-possibly-perhaps. It's the best I can do. I gaze towards the hotel. I think of him looking out across the water. Towards me.

We return to the shore. Small stones, sand and mud stick to my feet. I take off my soaked underpants. For a moment I'm naked. I dry myself with my T-shirt before putting the rest of my clothes on, brushing the stones off my feet as I put my socks and shoes on. My father dresses as though he's already dry. The consequence of this is that water emerges through his clothes in small patches. It is as though he's sprung a series of leaks. I am drier than him, but left with the sodden pair of green striped underpants I swam in and the damp T-shirt I used to dry myself. I hand my T-shirt to my father. He wipes his face and dries his hair then gives it back to me. I wonder what to do with it. I don't want to carry wet clothes in a cream-coloured taxi back to Bernau bei Berlin while listening to country and western music. I see the bin in the distance near the galleon at the children's playground we passed. I walk to it. I lift its black plastic lid and in an act of minor extravagance throw my T-shirt and underpants away. The lid springs shut, its wire spring glinting for a second as it does so. I return and stand next to my father. He is sitting on a tree stump. No words are exchanged between us. The silence is thickening. I can feel it pressing on my skin, now surrounding me, the wordlessness of the air between us, passing over us, this silence that is far from quiet as it enjoins the air to compress my arms and the top of my head. The pressure inside my skull increases. The joints in my fingers stiffen. My left hip jams. The sounds of birds in the trees arrive at my ears. Sound waves oscillate my eardrums. This is reality as it is. It is no more and no less than this.

I glance at my father. He is wet. He is cold. He is staring across the water at the Seeschloss Hotel. His eyes are ferocious. His body is motionless. His hands rest upon his lap. His legs are crossed. One foot is slightly raised. He has withdrawn into himself. He is at the place where no one can join him. How

can they? How can I? They have no right. I have no right.
He cannot be joined. Some things cannot be spoken. Some
things cannot be uttered. Some things cannot be shared.
Some things must be endured alone. There are no words.
There are no sounds. He sits on the tree stump. He is the
saddest man I have ever seen. He is the loneliest man I have
ever seen. My father. Hans.

5.2

Occasionally my mother and father took us swimming in the open-air pool in Llandrindod and, although my mother never ventured into the water, she always brought towels and sandwiches and orange squash. The pool was often busy in the middle of summer. That day it seemed particularly crowded and good-natured. The sun was out and bright.

As the afternoon wore on I saw my friend Heather sitting on the edge of the pool with her feet dangling over the side. For some reason I walked behind her and pushed her into the pool. It was the shallow end and she stood safely on the bottom of the pool up to her waist but she was shocked and she cried and when my father realised what I had done he screamed out, 'Come here, you little bastard,' and ran towards me with his face twisted up, and I ran away from him so quickly I enthralled myself, for the speed I could suddenly move at seemed incredible to me and I felt elated as I accelerated around the edge of the pool, the balls of my feet glancing against the ground, my legs moving quickly and with such strength it was as though they belonged to someone else. I weaved around people who were sunbathing on towels, past children jumping in and out of the water, past the long blue water slide at the pool's edge, my legs moving, increasingly confidently, my hips swivelling faster than they had ever moved before, until I was at the other end of the pool, which was now the deep end. I was so certain that I would get away and so thrilled at my new-found powers of speed that I was astonished when my father caught up with me and grabbed me from behind and lifted me into the air. 'I'm going to teach you a lesson you'll never forget,' he breathed into my ear and he carried me to the edge of the pool, grabbed hold of my arms and, as I fought and kicked at him, began to swing me round and round in circles as though I was a discus and he the thrower. When he let me go I was flung high into the air where I twisted this way and that before landing in the water with such force that it stung the side of my body and my breath was pushed out of me. Suddenly I was, for the first time in my life, in water that was out of my depth and as I couldn't swim I started to sink. When I surfaced I gulped at the pool's water, drinking it in volumes, as though I might swallow the whole pool to save myself, the stinging liquid hurting my throat and eyes, the taste of it making me retch.

Panic gripped me tight and spread through my body, a dark liquid pouring itself from somewhere inside me, an infernal spring cascading through me and invading me until it became all that was left of me. I thrashed at the water with all my might, hitting it repeatedly with my arms, my limbs desperate and flailing, like the cockroaches on the kitchen floor before they were cast into the fire, like the bludgeoned shimmering mackerel I would catch in the future. Then, as I began to sink I felt the terror increase further, the strange underwater sounds of the swimming pool hitting my ears, the colours of the water a strange diffused opalescent green, before I was enveloped, not knowing which way up my body was or where I was. And then I began to recede from myself and leave myself and I felt myself oddly begin to relax.

As I began to sink further the water pressed into my mouth and into my nose and ears, and the pressure became intolerable. Then, just as I began to inhale the water while I was under its surface, I felt a hand grab my arm and pull at it, lifting me back up above the surface, returning me to air, choking. I don't know who he was, this man, for there were no lifeguards at the pool, but he spoke kindly to me and then passed me to someone else who helped me to the side of the pool and pushed me over its edge onto the dry land. There I lay on my front and pressed my face as hard as I could into the solid ground, my forehead absorbing the heat of the warm, gritty concrete edge of the pool, a shrine of peace and safety.

I felt the panic pass through me and begin to subside and I felt myself gradually come back to myself, returning from wherever I had been. I felt the sun beating on my back and I started shivering hard, strange involuntary convulsions that shook my teeth and body. My heart beat ferociously as though it was trying to force itself out of my chest and onto the side of the pool to gain its freedom. It was as though it had a life of its own, my heart, that it wanted to break its cage and rupture my chest and sit alongside me, free from the terrors my body had inflicted on it. Then my stomach muscles suddenly spasmed, pushing them into my tummy and against the front of my spine, and I was sick. I spewed water with saliva on its top and then some food and then I shat myself and then I pissed myself, the thin brown liquid tracing its journey down the inside of my legs and collecting in a pool beside me. As I lay there, my face still to the ground, my heart leaping in my ribcage, huge shudders that were beyond my control overwhelmed me. It was as though I were a caterpillar arcing as my body became possessed by giant peristaltic contractions. More water came out of me and I became aware of a silence that had descended on the poolside, a hush at my public humiliation, a thickening of the air, a fear of what had just happened.

Eventually I stood up and walked to the other end of the pool on my own, where people pointed at me. I went and lay down on the concrete bench that leant against a dirty concrete wall, under the branches of an overhanging tree, and pulled my knees up to my chest. Sometime later I saw my father swimming up and down the pool on his own, steady lengths of crawl, one arm extending over the other, the strong, easy rhythm of an experienced swimmer, his head flicking sideways to his right on every other stroke as he sucked in oxygen.

Afterwards he refused to talk to me. In turn I refused to speak to him or anyone else for days and then I refused to eat. I lay in my room as supper was called but refused to come downstairs to consume it. My brothers and sisters would be sent upstairs each evening to tell me to come down but I refused to join the family at the kitchen table. Eventually my father would force me to the table by coming upstairs to my bedroom, dragging me out of my bed and carrying me downstairs to the table, placing me in a chair and watching me. 'I'm not moving until you bloody well eat,' he would say, but I knew that he was far too impatient to outlast my already strong will. I dug in for the long haul and just stared at him. 'I mean it. I'm staying until you put something in that stomach of yours, and stop staring at me.' I would stare at my food, then at him, my stomach in a strange, confused state – both ravenously hungry yet unable to eat – as food suddenly seemed repulsive to me. 'This is ridiculous!' my father would shout. 'Ridiculous!' And then he would storm out of the room only minutes after having claimed that he would remain until I ate. 'I've got much better things to do,' he would say as he left the room, exhaling in exasperation. My mother would sit next to me and cut up my food on my plate, put it on a fork and hold it next to my mouth, but I would tighten my lips so that nothing could pass between them and then silently go back upstairs. I wouldn't eat much for days, or talk. People commented on how thin I was becoming.

I would crawl under my bed and lie there, sniffing the reassuring smell of the accumulated dust on the bedroom floor, or settle inside a cupboard, my back pressed against its sides for hours at a time. I would disappear on long walks alone, along the River Ithon, up the steep sides of Castle Hill. Sometimes I would slide down the banks of the Ithon and walk into the river. I would watch the water flow past my legs. Occasionally I would walk into the water further, over the slippery rocks on the riverbed, at times as far as my waist, feeling the current pressing against me as it surged against my hips and waist, its force an unstoppable and continuous flow of life that talked to me in gurgles and made the muscles of my legs ache. At other times I would ensconce myself in a hedge, using my coat to protect myself against its thorns, and sit watching birds and spiders and ants and occasionally in summer the luminous violet and greens of a dragonfly. Or I would lie flat in a ditch and let insects crawl over me or climb a tree and sit in it for hours so that sometimes birds would land close to me. When it rained in summer I would concentrate hard and let the water drip slowly down the back of my neck, feeling it gradually wet my back.

In the moment of being hurled into the water and then left to nearly drown, a part of me was fractured. A wild horse can be broken within an afternoon and will remain tamed for the rest of its life, and I was nothing like a wild horse – just a particularly small and timid child. A piece of me had been snapped apart in those minutes in the pool and I knew it. It made me unable to eat properly, unable to ingest nourishment, something that I still in later life have not resolved. I still avoid pools. I still have nightmares about drowning and for many years assumed I would die this way. The event inscribed itself onto my psyche so that I occasionally wake with the sense of asphyxiation, the reflexes of my body violently kicking and pushing and expelling the imagined intrusion of water. It has been said that drowning is a peaceful way to die but that was not my experience. My body retched and protested and fought the water with all its might. Afterwards I learned to avoid my father as much as I could. And I began to hate him.

It arrived inside me, this hate, like a dark stone. It became my poison. It eroded my life and punished me far more severely than him. It denuded me, shrivelled my spirit, made me mean and secretive, kept me away from others. It meant I had no friends, that I became marked out, that I was not, as everyone kept telling me, like the other children. I became a stranger to myself, not recognising why I did the things I did, fighting and failing and shouting and screaming and refusing and constantly breaking things and falling over and lying in bed for days at a time and starving myself and clenching my teeth and never smiling and enduring a sharp unremitting loneliness and moods so bleak I felt them press in on me until I wasn't there. And as thin as a wafer.

5.3

We walk to Friedrichstraße and stand on the platform from where my father left Berlin, leaving his mother and everything else behind him. We stand for a while. 'There were Alsatians,' says my father. 'My mother waved me off.' I look at his face. It's calm. 'I carried a carpet and a watch.' This is the place. Its rails curve and so does its platforms. I have often wondered if I was meant to be with him to hold his hand as he waved goodbye to Ruth. Perhaps some events stand outside time.

We watch trains depart, look at the station's steel and glass roof, buy coffees and sip them on the platform. We take the S1 train to Oranienburg. Two electricians board and sit opposite us dressed in the same work clothes. Their achromatic grey trousers have coal-black patches at their knees. Both wear belts with tools on them. A woman with a pushchair boards at Nordbahnhof with two young boys. One of them sits in the chair while the other hangs onto its back. The train passes through Humboldthain and Wollankstraße and then heads into the countryside through Frohnau and Borgsdorf and Lehnitz, the land cold, the earth bare. We arrive at Oranienburg station. We walk down steps then through a tiled underpass. The electricians pass us, their gait purposeful. There's a gathering of young people outside the station entrance. The schools have just finished. They wait at a series of bus stops to take their buses home. They hold bags of books. Some of them cluster together talking, others stand alone. Some drink from paper cups. Occasionally a parent stops to pick one of them up, the teenager sliding in through the car door fluidly, sitting in the seat, the car pulling away quickly, the parent's eyes set upon the road ahead.

Across the road there is a signpost with several signs on it pointing in different directions. One points to the town centre, the others to the surrounding villages. Another of the signs is for Sachsenhausen concentration camp. It's a 2.5-kilometre walk, the signs tell us. We follow the signs, passing a long line of shops then under a railway bridge. We walk for some time alongside a major road and against the wind, turn left along sheltered urban side streets, pass several blocks of recently built flats, and then along a cobbled street with smart detached houses on either side. Oranienburg was the administrative centre for all the concentration camps. All the houses here are well maintained. We pass along a road with a wall built from concrete blocks on one side, the walls of Sachsenhausen concentration camp.

Sachsenhausen was built in 1936. It was the first camp to be constructed and was initially built as a punishment centre. It also served as a training camp for the SS, the Schutzstaffel. Several ideas were first tried here: the triangular shape of the compound, the number of huts for prisoners, the shape and order of the way prisoners should stand at roll calls, various ways of execution, various ways of incineration, the minimum number of machine-gun posts necessary to enforce imprisonment.

We come to the camp entrance. It is set inside the perimeter walls. We walk through the gates with their welded black steel sign on them: ARBEIT MACHT FREI. I touch the letters with my fingers as we pass through. The welding around each individual letter is crude, and they're smaller than I imagined they would be. The entrance is through an arch that has a machine-gun placement above it, as well as what was the commandant's offices.

And then we are inside. Initially it seems surprisingly small. Each of the perimeter walls can be clearly seen from the entrance. In front of each of the walls there's a death strip, the '*Verbotene Zone*', where '*Eintritt verboten es wird geschossen*'. Barbed wire has been laid in rolls. 'It won't be the original, the original would have rusted away by now,' says my father. There are two wooden barracks to the right of the entrance. We walk towards them. The originals were partially burnt in an arson attack in 1992. The huts have been reconstructed using the remains. We walk through the doors into one of them. Behind a clear screen are rows of bunk beds with three levels. They are much smaller than I expected, these three-level bunk beds that are ingrained in my mind.

In the centre of the hut are two small rooms, one with a line of brown toilet bowls. There is a cordon saying no entry. My father and I duck underneath it and stand in the room. Hundreds of people would have used them at one time. The other small room contains footbaths, also made from brown ware. We stand in that too. A sign tells us that men were drowned in these footbaths by guards keeping their heads under the water by standing on them.

We leave the huts and walk into the punishment block where prisoners were taken to be tortured. We push the main door open and see rows of cells on either side of a corridor. Each has a window letting in natural light, and a bed. The door of each cell is covered in metal. They are held open against the corridor's wall by a catch. The doors are thick and have a tiny eyeglass in them. My father presses one of the catches and releases the door. He pulls it slowly out into the corridor, and then, while still holding onto it, walks backwards. Taking tiny steps to ensure the bottom of the door does not hit his feet, he reverses into the cell the door is joined onto. I accompany him. He pulls the door to. We stand in the cell. We take it in turns to lean forwards and gaze through the door's eyeglass. It's a fish-eyed eyeglass but is so scratched that I can see nothing through it. We stand for a minute then open the door and leave. My father pushes the door against the wall of the corridor and puts it back on its latch. The air in the block is cold. A sign says, 'Indescribable suffering took place in these cells.'

We walk to the end of the block. Most of the original cell block has been pulled down. The section we have just walked through with thirty or so cells in it is the remains of a larger punishment block. We walk out of it to see three poles in the ground where people were hung by their arms, after being lifted from behind. Jean Améry described what happened to him:

The hook gripped into the shackle that held my hands together behind my back. Then I was raised with the chain until I hung a metre over the floor. In such a position, or rather, when hanging this way, with your hands behind your back, for a short time you can hold at a half oblique through muscular force. During these few minutes when you are already expending your utmost strength, when sweat has already appeared on your forehead and lips, and you're breathing in gasps ... all your life is gathered in a single limited area of the body ... but this cannot last long even with people who have a strong physical constitution. As for me I had to give up rather quickly. And now there was a crackling and splintering in my shoulders that my body has not forgotten until this hour. The balls sprang from their sockets. My body caused luxation; I fell into a void and now hung by my dislocated arms, which had been torn from high behind and were now twisted over my head. Torture, from Latin *torquere*, to twist.[4]

Later he goes on to note:

> ... the boundaries of my body are the boundaries of myself ... the border violation of myself by the other can neither be neutralized by the expectation of help nor rectified through resistance ...[5]

Which logically leads to the observation that, 'after the first blow I lose my trust in the world'.

This trust, he goes on to say, can never return. It leads him to write with inexorable logic the following note, while living with his wife in the Austrian city of the 'salt fortress', Salzburg.

> *To the Salzburg police authorities,*
> *Salzburg, October 16, 1978*
> To the pertinent police authorities
> Dear Gentlemen:
> I, the undersigned,
> Hans Maier (yclept: Jean Améry)
> Author, resident in 56, Avenue Coghen, Brussels
> Hereby declare that I voluntarily, in full possession of
> my mental faculties, bring my life to an end.[6]

We walk past the running track where men were sent to run to test the durability of military boots until they dropped with exhaustion.

We walk towards the execution trench where men were executed by firing squad. Suddenly the camp seems much larger than I first realised. It takes us a long time to cross the camp from one side to another. Later I find out that it is 1,000 acres. We reach the trench and walk down a long slope until we are standing at the point where people were shot. Sawn-off tree trunks are behind us. In front of us is a small building where people were kept waiting before they were murdered.

We walk back up the slope and out. There is a huge white structure in front of us. We walk into it. Inside it are the remains of the gas chambers and the incinerators that were installed in 1943. The ovens of the incinerators are small, the doors are made from cast iron. Lying on the remains of the ovens are three stretchers with long handles. They are a particular shape. They are the type that were used to carry dead bodies from the gas chamber to the ovens. They are long and thin and have long handles. I walk to one of them and put my hand around each handle. I lift it. How strange to lift such an object. It is light. There is the thinnest layer of white dust covering it, and everything else too. I don't know where it has come from, this dust. Perhaps from the drying cement. Perhaps it's been placed here. The large canopy above us has stopped all wind. We walk over to some foundations. These are the foundations of gas chambers. Their footprints are small. We stand together on one of them. We are the only people here.

We leave and walk out through the entrance. There's ice on the ground. We walk alongside the wall, past the machine-gun towers, past the barbed wire, past the gates with '*Arbeit Macht Frei*'. We walk to the visitors' café. I ask for two coffees. My voice is so quiet that the man serving me can't hear me. I repeat the order. The man leans towards me. My voice has disappeared. The man says,

> People come from all over the world to visit Sachsenhausen. Then they come in here and they are all in such difficulties. All I can do is get their coffee right. Please tell me your order again.

An angel is serving in the coffee shop.

We drink our carefully made coffees and then leave. We pass the houses on either side of the cobbled street, which it turns out were originally built for SS officers and their families. We walk through Oranienburg and take the train home through the countryside back to Berlin. We are both silent. My father looks at me.

> *Do you understand now?*
> What?
> *How lucky I am.*

That night I wake terrified. My hands feel huge and are burning. Each feels as though it is the size of my body. I should not have touched the stretcher's handles. Touching such an evil thing is wrong. I am gripped with sweat. What was I doing? Why did I do it? What's wrong with me?

And then the storm arrives. It hurls itself onto my body as though it is a gale. It urges me to jump out of the window onto the street below. It impinges itself upon my body. It inscribes itself on the surface of me. It enters my entrails and spine. I stand and walk to the window and look down. The terrors have come again. They are gripping me. They pin me. They push me so hard to jump that I have to use all my will to resist. I have an overwhelming desire to leave the world. My body shakes. My head feels as if it is going to explode. I can hear my heart banging away chaotically in my chest. The blood in my eardrums sounds like the loudest sound. I do what I do when this happens. I lie down. On the ground. I curl up. I bring my knees to my chest. I wrap my arms around my shins. I pull my head to my body. With all my force I breathe as the Buddhists have taught me to. One breath at a time. Concentrating on the area below my nostrils and above my upper lip. Cold air into my lungs. Warm air out.

In. Out. In. Out. In. Out. In. Out. In. Out. In. Anicca. Anicca. Anicca. Anicca. Anicca. All things will pass. All things will pass. All things will pass. All things will pass. All things will pass.

5.4

I stand up. I lie down. I stand up. I lie down. I stand
up. I lie down. I stand up. I lie down. I stand up. I lie
down. I stand up. I lie down. I stand up. I lie down.
I stand up. I lie down. I stand up. I lie down. I stand
up. I lie down. I stand up. I lie down. I stand up. I lie
down. I stand up. I lie down. I stand up. I lie down.
I stand up. I lie down. I stand up. I lie down. I stand
up. I lie down. I stand up. I lie down. I stand up. I lie
down. I stand up. I lie down. I stand up. I lie down.
I stand up. I lie down. I stand up. I lie down. I stand up.

I can't stand up. I stand up. I can't stand up. I stand up.
I can't stand up. I stand up. I can't stand up. I stand up.
I can't stand up. I stand up. I can't stand up. I stand up.
I can't stand up. I stand up. I can't stand up. I stand up.
I can't stand up. I stand up. I can't stand up. I stand up.
I can't stand up. I stand up. I can't stand up. I stand up.
I can't stand up. I stand up. I can't stand up. I stand up.
I can't stand up. I stand up. I can't stand up. I stand up.
I can't stand up. I stand up. I can't stand up. I stand up.
I can't stand up. I stand up. I can't stand up. I stand up.

I lie down. Face down. I stand up. I can't stand up.
I lie down. Face down. I stand up. I can't stand up.
I lie down. Face down. I stand up. I can't stand up.
I lie down. Face down. I stand up. I can't stand up.
I lie down. Face down. I stand up. I can't stand up.
I lie down. Face down. I stand up. I can't stand up.
I lie down. Face down. I stand up. I can't stand up.
I lie down. Face down. I stand up. I can't stand up.

We are leaving the Grimm's Hotel. I take the lift down to the hotel's car park located in the basement to collect the car. The car park was built within the foundations of the hotel so it's difficult to get out of and I spend a long time manoeuvring the car, its old diesel engine quickly filling up the small space with fumes, constricting my throat, making me gag, despite the car windows being closed. Eventually I manage to get the car up the ramp to the exit, a steel security gate. After winding down the window while holding my breath I press the security code and wait for the steel shutter to rise. It takes a long time to wind itself upwards, this steel shutter, and because it is at the top of a ramp the car's nose points upwards towards it. Shutter lifted, I drive out and for a moment face only the revealed sky before levelling off and turning onto Seydelstraße where I park outside the hotel. The fumes are still catching my throat.

My father emerges from the hotel entrance carrying his case, loads the car and then we set off, turning left immediately onto Neue Grünstraße then into Ritterstraße and then out along the wide Lindenstraße with its array of architecture, recessed concrete shops with bright signs, modern glass, early nineteenth-century apartments with small leaded windows. Contradictory architecture serrates the street, Berlin's scar tissue from the blanket bombing by the Allies and my neighbour Bryn. We make our way towards the edge of the Tiergarten where, just before we turn left at the Brandenburg Gate, the Reichstag is directly in front of us.

I remember watching it burn down.

The Reichstag?

You could see it for miles. Smoke lasted for days.

Did you ever see Hitler?

Hitler was always parading around in his cars. Volkswagens.

Or Mercedes.

Which is why you hated those cars?

What do you think?

What did Hitler look like?

He had similar colouring to you when you were a child.

Really?

He had reddish hair. And it fell to one side, like yours.

Did you salute him?

I hailed him.

You gave him the Nazi salute?

Primary schools were sent out to do it.

Even Jewish children?

We all hailed Hitler.

During the war VW used forced Jewish slave labour.

Mercedes too.

Everyone knows that.

We drive through the Tiergarten. The linden trees crowd the ground. They are without their leaves, their bark glimmers. We pass around the victory column, the Siegessäule, with its golden statue shining at its top and where one can, by climbing the stairs inside its column, catch a glimpse of its wings from below.

Hitler had the Siegessäule moved.

Did he?

It used to be by the Reichstag. He had it moved and then made it taller.

How did he do that?

He had an extra section added onto the bottom; you can still see it. It's paler. Idiot.

We pass down Hofjägerallee, turn right along Stülerstraße to Budapester Straße, where we arrive at the elephant gate entrance to Berlin's zoo. There's no official parking here so I edge the car onto the pavement. My father gets out and walks over to one of the entrance's stone elephants. I switch the car's hazard lights on. He is partially lit by blinking orange light. I join him.

I often came here with my father.

Did you?

And with Toni. We used to walk through the Tiergarten. We stood by these elephants.

Was your father kind?

Kind?

He looks around. He hesitates. His head bends to the ground. His chest sinks. His knees stoop. His jaw locks.

He was very kind.

I see his memories coming towards him and then they envelop him. They are like a rush of the fiercest wind. They pass into him and then through him, the squall of them fighting him, making his body tremble before imperceptibly shrinking him.

This was our favourite place.

Pinned down, his feet have taken root. The car's orange warning lights continue to make their regular blink. People around the gate are gesticulating, telling us we shouldn't be parking here, but I feel entitled to these few minutes and so ignore them. Almost silently he whispers,

We held each other's hand.

He moves back towards the car, taking the tiniest footsteps. I open the door for him. He lowers himself into the seat.

We set off, driving down the long, straight Kaiserdamm to the ring road and then, surprisingly quickly, the city begins to fade away. I stop for diesel again and my father waits quietly in the car as I get out and pay. There's a strong cold wind blowing across the forecourt. I buy cups of black coffee and two packets of chocolate, one Toffifees, the other Knoppers, and then we set out for Holland. My father is leaving the city for the last time. He knows he won't come back and so do I. These are the final moments as we pull out of this petrol station. He is quiet for a long time before he speaks, and when he does Berlin has disappeared.

You know . . .

Yes?

I . . .

Yes?

What?

You were saying?

These Toffifees.

Yes?

Delicious.

You think so?

Never had them before. Toffee. Chocolate.

What about the Knoppers?

The Knoppers are all right. I prefer the Toffifees.

I look over at the passenger seat. My father has opened all the
chocolate and is eating it quietly. The tray of Toffifees rests
on his legs, the packet of Knoppers is in his hand, the coffee
is in the cup holder.

My Uncle Fritz committed suicide in Amsterdam.

Another suicide?

Sometime in 1942. Toni told me about it when she visited.

How?

He drank poison. About to be deported by the Nazis. He's
the man in the photograph of our shop after it was smashed
on Kristallnacht. Not sure why he was there. I liked him
enormously.

The Autobahn stretches far into the distance.

> Three suicides?
> *Yes.*
> Your father and your grandfather. And your uncle?
> *That's correct.*
> Then just you and your mother left?
> *And my grandmother.*
> And then you went on the *Kindertransport*.
> *Yes.*
> Your family gradually disappeared?
> *You could say that.*

The car is suddenly crammed full of ghosts. They have arrived again. I feel them pressing onto my skin. I realise again how remarkable my father has been to have survived the gradual loss of his family, his friends, his surroundings and his country. All these suicides. I realise too that I have accompanied him as he has struggled to deal with the consequences of what happened to him. His tempers and furies, his criticisms, his drives, his pride in physical extremes, his incessant activity were his way of coping with these things. And perhaps he felt he wanted me to toughen up in case I had to deal with them too. My obvious fragility frightened him as much as it frightened me. He wanted me to be prepared to be able to deal with not what *might* happen, but what eventually *would* happen. I realise what an immense privilege it is to be his son.

You're amazing.
I'm not.
To have endured.
Endured?
It's been a privilege to be your son.
What are you talking about?

I press the accelerator to the car's floor. It incrementally gathers speed until it goes faster than it's ever been, in the fast lane of this Autobahn with no speed limits. I wind the windows down. Freezing air rushes into the car, tyre noise from the road fills our heads, the engine howls in protest. We pass cars with caravans, lorries, vans, minibuses, cars. My hands become cold on the steering wheel. I concentrate as much as I can: at this speed the car feels delicate, as though

273

it's running on tiptoes, each change of camber in the road shifting it around. Suddenly, above the wind blowing through the window my father says something.

Fuck the Nazis.
What did you say?
Fuck the Nazis.
Fuck the Nazis?
Fuck the Nazis.

I look quickly over at him. The wind is blowing his hair around but he's relaxed at this speed, the hint of danger energising him. His face breaks into a smile that creases it, revealing his lower teeth, bent and crooked. Suddenly he laughs, short stabs of sound against the wind. As the car approaches its maximum speed he leans over, takes the cup of coffee from the car's cup holder, sips it and proclaims,

Fuck them.

5.5

My father's favourite occupation was to walk through the Cambrian Mountains that surrounded Llandrindod. He would drag his children with him, as well as friends and any distant relative who might be visiting. He could walk for miles at a pace that was far too fast for everyone else and spent his time cajoling us to keep up with him: 'Come on! It's not too far now! You can do it!', as though we were on the verge of failing basic military training rather than out for a walk.

During these walks the weather would often 'turn', for this part of Wales is where the winds from the west, the westerlies, are abruptly slowed by its mountains. While travelling across the Atlantic and the Irish Sea the westerlies pick up both water vapour and speed so that when they hit the first high ground they come to, the Cambrian Mountains, the air rushes quickly upwards, cools rapidly and discharges its collected water vapour as rain. As the westerlies move quickly, so the weather changes rapidly. And as they are the predominant weather system of the British Isles they govern much of the weather in this part of Wales, which, consequently, can shift from a tender warmth to a fierce driving rain and then back again in the space of a quarter of an hour. My father taught us how to manage the weather's rapid changeability by wearing many layers of clothing – shirts, jumpers, coats, thin nylon raincoats – so that we could maintain our bodies at a constant temperature. If we needed a rest he would find the lee of a hillock or a wall for us to escape the wind, sometimes encouraging us to lie flat on the short springy grass so that the wind passed above us and where, while it screeched and blew, he would peel oranges, handing out their segments to us, their juice as luscious as nectar, the dimpled orange peel bright and shining against the dull grass. He taught us to read the weather by watching the direction of clouds, first establishing which ones were moving away and which coming towards us. To do this he would periodically stop, pick up a few blades of grass and throw them in the air to see in which direction they fell after the wind had caught them, or he would lick his finger and hold it up into the air above his head. 'The side of your finger that goes cold first tells you which way the wind is coming from,' he would tell us, as if he hadn't told us this a thousand times before. 'So that tells you that clouds are moving towards us and which away.'

He was adept at reading the weather – 'It's going to rain soon, quite heavily but not for long. We'd better put our coats on.' And indeed this would be what happened. And during the summer, while on the summit of a hill, in the bright air, with views stretching around us in a complete circle as far as our eyes could see, we would lie together on our backs on the sheep-eaten grass for an hour or more without speaking, each of us lost in silent contemplation.

He was, though, oddly useless at directions and without

fail would get lost, so that a walk that was announced as 'two hours at the most' would go on for four or five or even six hours, and by the time we got home we were always starving hungry and bad-tempered. Then, if it had been cold, to warm us up he would make us each a cup of Horlicks, the drink he had lived off for years and that he drank on an industrial scale. He bought it in huge catering packs the size of small oil drums, which had even been allotted their own cupboard in the kitchen – the *Horlicks* cupboard.

Because of him, we travelled across the land's topography, touching objects from its history, its rocks and hills carved through by meandering rivers, its ancient sites of battles and struggles, its unusually high concentration of ruined castles, its sparse population, its hill farms with their stone walls, this little-known county of Radnor itself part of the ancient Welsh Marches, the area that for centuries fell between the English and Welsh borders and so was a territory of its own, ruled by the Marcher Lords under their own laws.

Such was the authority of the Marcher Lords that those convicted of crimes in England or Wales could move to the Marches, claim 'Marcher Liberties' and become free. The area was, for hundreds of years, a haven outside the legal jurisdiction of either of its surrounding countries. It was a frontier land where not only criminals arrived but also those from across the sea – Bretons, Flemings, Normans, those from Wexford, Wicklow and Dalkeg as well as the English and Welsh. This history perhaps accounts for the still fierce local scepticism of authority, the social status given to those who 'beat the system', the drunkenness, lawlessness and strikingly violent fights on Saturday nights as well as the characteristic looks of many local families, with their dark shining eyes and small, fiercely strong bodies. The local phrase we heard often as children was,

> Neither Wales nor England,
> Just Radnorsheer.

Sometimes my father would walk us away from the hills and instead follow the banks of the Ithon. We would walk along its edges for hours, through fields, past hawthorn bushes and woods of oak and beech, along steep paths that climbed high above the river and then across it on stepping stones where it was shallow. At other times we walked under the river's bridges, wading through the cold, clear water with our trousers rolled up, carrying our shoes and socks, small shoals of minnows clearly visible as they nibbled at our feet, the smoothed stones of the riverbed slippery with thick luminous-green algae, the rare flash of a kingfisher on the bank, the sound of finches and crows in the bordering trees, the trout, grayling and pike unseen but present in the deeper water. Our walk would pass St Cewydd's Church at Disserth, situated some miles away from Llandrindod where the water pools deeply black, the flowing river seemingly coming to a standstill, and so opaque, and where, we had heard said, that due to the specific confluence of the river's currents, the bottom was unreachable. As we approached this pool we would move away from the river's edge to give it a wide berth, partly because it was rumoured that a woman accused of being a witch had been ceremonially drowned there while the area was under the Mortimers' rule. We would then cross the narrow road bridge that passes above the top of the pool, past its railings covered in flaking drake-green paint, and where, at the centre, was a cast-iron coat of arms of the old county of Radnor, the heads of three black boars on a white background, itself a reference to the Mortimers' coat of arms.

My father had settled in Llandrindod as a doctor, where he worked particularly conscientiously, and it was because of this that as a child I was often stopped by people in the street and asked for medical advice. 'Do you think this is serious?' people would say, before listing their symptoms as though as a child I was capable of making informed decisions, and even assuming I had miraculously gained the prerequisite medical training by the age of nine. I would at first reply by saying that I didn't know but as people generally persisted until I gave a decision I learned to emulate my father's speech rhythms and copy his phrases and so found myself saying, 'If it gets worse get it seen to, otherwise you should be fine', or, 'Try taking some aspirin', and sometimes, 'If your temperature doesn't fall within twenty-four hours and it's still swollen then ring the surgery.' People would often touch my shoulder or press my hand and ask, 'Are you the doctor's boy?' and if I said 'Yes', which I usually did, they would follow with, 'Your father saved my son', or, 'Here's half a crown, just tell your father thank you from Mrs Price', or, 'If it wasn't for your dad my mother would have died.' Once I was given a large navel orange by an elderly woman who rushed out of Giles's vegetable shop to present it to me, exclaiming while she shook her head and handed me the surprising fruit: 'Your father. Pulling that boy out of the River Ithon yesterday. At Disserth. By St Cewydd's too.' That boy. In the river. The one my father would not mention.

5.6

We drive for hours on the Autobahn, eventually reaching Bad Oeynhausen where we stop so that my father can eat a frankfurter from the same garage we pulled into on the way to Berlin ('Oh go on! Let's! We need a break, and they were absolutely delicious!') We stand again on the garage forecourt and watch the *Waschstraße* in action with its promise of *Sauger- und Pflege – Dienstleistungen mit Qualität*. The green-clothed car washers move around the line of dirty cars as though in a continual dance. My father eats two frankfurters with mustard again ('Might as well go the whole hog!') before we drive further west, leaving the Autobahn at Bad Bentheim where we stop again at the Bentheimer Hof. Here the same woman with silver wire-framed glasses serves us coffee, asks my father questions in German and receives from him, as we leave, a large tip. We walk quickly down the gravel path opposite the Bentheimer Hof's entrance and gaze at the Pyramide in the woods ('Bloody odd, whichever way you look at it') then drive into Holland towards Amsterdam. My father relaxes once we've crossed the border into Holland. His body slopes in the car seat. He wiggles his toes and feet. He tells me animatedly about his time in Wales as a doctor, the joy of its countryside, how he loves Llandrindod, the village he has lived in for over fifty years, that the *Kindertransport* had taken him away from one life but given him a new, unexpected one, one that he couldn't ask more from. His voice lifts as he talks about Radnorshire, about Llandegley Rocks and Castle Hill, how he's learning Welsh, how he has more friends than he thought he'd ever have. He talks about his ten grandchildren, as well as his two great-grandchildren, in detail, revels in memories of paragliding over the Elan Valley and the Black Mountains.

> *When the wind runs across the ridge on a warm day I can soar on the heated currents, the warm air lifting me up, hundreds of feet high. It's most exhilarating.*

He points out that many people on the *Kindertransport* have made significant contributions to British life, that there were four Nobel Prize winners among his peers on the trains – 'One for every two and a half thousand of us' – and discusses in detail the cancer centre he helped start with my mother: 'The Bracken Trust. You know the local community keeps that place going with donations only, isn't that utterly remarkable?' He reminds me of the many trips with medical supplies he helped organise to Bosnia during the civil war in Yugoslavia, how he visited schools to tell children about his childhood, how people in Llandrindod made the trips to Bosnia too, and donated money, about the wheel that fell off a lorry he was on in France, 'that bloody well passed by my window on the motorway', and how the driver miraculously managed to get safely onto the hard shoulder. He tells me that when he received his MBE from the

Queen she asked him if he knew what it was for and he replied that he wasn't exactly sure, so she had to tell him – it was for his work taking medicine to Bosnia.

We drive into Amsterdam where we park close to the Amsterdam Centraal, the city's main railway station. We walk through crowds and stand next to the long, curved brick façade, gazing up at its tall ornamental brick towers, noticing the restored golden hands on each of its twin clocks, the detail of its intricately eaved doors, the windows in its array of tiered roofs. The decoration on the top of the towers echoes the fenestrations of a medieval cathedral. Travel using religious iconography, main stations its cathedrals.

I stood here with the other Kindertransportees.

Here?

More or less. A group of women led us into a square near the palace. They gave us hot chocolate. They wore white aprons.

We trace the route he and his fellow *Kindertransportees* walked along, the broad Nieuwezijds Voorburgwal that ends at the square in front of the Koninklijk Paleis.

It's here we all drank the cups of hot chocolate.

Later, we decide to drink, as a miniature but symbolic act of triumph, a hot chocolate opposite the Koninklijk Paleis ourselves. While we are looking for a suitable café to enact this ritual we pass a display of some one hundred or so navel oranges on a market stall and I am suddenly reminded about the strange present that I had been given from Giles the greengrocer all those years ago. And so I remember the boy at Disserth and finally ask my father what had happened. Nearly fifty years later the memory is still painfully acute for him but finally, and slowly, with his eyes clouding and while sipping a cup of steaming hot chocolate in a white-ware cup outside Café De Zwart, he tells me what had happened that day at the River Ithon as the chattering crowds swirled on the Dam and the lights bounced off the Paleis.

I received a call to say that a boy was in difficulties in St Cewydd's pool below Disserth Bridge. I drove there as fast as I could. When I arrived a group of twenty or so children and seven or eight adults were standing on the bank. The adults were too frightened to enter the pool. Idiots. I jumped off the bridge. I kept diving under the water until I found him. He was very near the riverbank. He was sitting upright with his legs folded under him. He was kneeling on the riverbed. His hair floated above him. The top of his head was only a few inches below the river's surface. As I swam towards him, perhaps due to the river's currents, or perhaps due to the movement of the water I was making, as though having seen me, he lifted his arm in recognition.

At this point my father leans forward slightly and I notice his piercing and faraway gaze come over him.

He seemed to offer his hand as a greeting. I extended my hand, took hold of his and we shook hands underwater. And I thought, against my common sense and against everything I knew from my medical training, that he might be still alive. It was only when I lifted him above the Ithon's surface and then struggled to get him onto the bank that I knew he was drowned. The movement of his arm had just been one of those things. I tried to resuscitate him. Eventually the ambulance arrived.

The rumour that I had heard at the school gates that summer afternoon was that my father had pulled a boy from the river. He had, I was told, leapt off the bridge at Disserth into the black water of St Cewydd's pool while others had stood by too frightened to enter its black depths. As I was only ten at the time, and given the ambiguity of the words 'pulled from the river', I assumed that my father had pulled the boy out alive and so when I got home I asked my father proudly at the kitchen table, while we were eating tea, about what had happened. Before my question was finished, and saying nothing, my father pushed his chair back sharply from the table, stood up and, leaving his food half eaten, walked outside into the garden. Through the kitchen window we watched him begin to split wood with his axe, his face set in a rictus grimace, his powerful shoulders rhythmically swinging the axe high into the air before bringing it down with tremendous force, splitting each log into pieces.

We finish the hot chocolate, eat the accompanying *stroop-wafels*, place our empty cups onto their saucers and walk back down Nieuwezijds Voorburgwal to Amsterdam Centraal. We return to the car and drive to the Hook of Holland. We stop to look at the statue by Frank Meisler situated outside the Hook's terminal, dedicated to the *Kindertransport* and entitled 'Channel Crossing to Life'. That night we stay up talking in the *Stena Britannica*'s Lounge-Restaurant and as the ship leaves the Hook of Holland my father's spirits lift further. He tells me about meeting my mother while he was in the SAS in Malaysia, how she was a nurse in Kuala Terengganu who needed some medicines, how he proposed to her the day he met her and how she had replied, 'Ask me in a month', and then how they got married, about my birth in Kuala Lumpur, about various car crashes, including the time he smashed his MG so badly that he was knocked unconscious. 'When I came round I was lying in a monsoon gutter holding the ripped-off steering wheel in my hand. Bloody MGs. Very badly built.'

Later my father sleeps soundly in our cabin as we cross the North Sea, the sound of the engines below us making the cabin hum. I see him with his white duvet up around his neck, his mouth relaxed, his breathing regular, his skin pink. He does not get up to wake me in the night.

We get up early to watch the *Stena Britannica*'s arrival at Parkeston Quay, standing on the rear deck of the ship as it sails past the container ships docked at Felixstowe, the row of blackbird cranes still patiently loading and unloading containers in what amounts to a ceaseless operation. As our ship towers above Harwich we notice the detail of the town from this height, how it is laid out on this eastern edge of Britain, how it was the perfect location for the old Royal Navy Dockyard with the deep water on two sides of its small headland, how it was my father's first view of freedom.

The estuaries of the Stour and Orwell wrinkle in the dawn's air as they join, their currents stirring the water. 'I want to catch the train home from here,' says my father. 'I want to do this final piece of the journey by train. I did say that when we left Wales, didn't I?' 'You did say that,' I reply. 'Shall I come with you to Liverpool Street?' I ask. 'If you like,' says my father before continuing,

I want to walk from the ship to the railway station in private, actually. I want to carry my case, too.

And so after the ropes of the ship have been coiled and thrown onto the quay, and after the ship has been moored by its chains and pulled to the edge of the docks with its winches, I go down to the car deck on my own and drive from the ship to Harwich International railway station and park the car, which I will pick up later. I walk to the platform to wait for the train to London. My father arrives from the ship after me. I see him emerge onto Platform One through the white doors of the station building. There is a lightness to his step and he is standing upright. I watch him walk to the flower bell located on the station wall. I see him place both hands upon it. I watch him bend his head to it.

We take the train to Liverpool Street together, sitting on the moss-green prickly train seats while it ambles nonchalantly along the small coastal branch line. On our right is the Stour estuary and in the distance, on the other side of the water, meadows dip into it, their banks autumn-green and often covered in trees. The train passes through Wrabness and as the estuary is tidal, and as the tide is out, dark acres of estuarine mud are revealed, patterned in the shape of rippled water, darkly shining. Here, small red clay Roman ampoules are occasionally found on the surface. The fields on our left have been ploughed, the brown earth turned over in regular lines, the tyres from the tractor have indented the ground. We pass gulls and waders with their long straight beaks and, at Manningtree, a colony of swans, two of whom fly past the train, their long necks stretched out before them.

The train stops at Colchester, having passed industrial estates and an old coal depot that is now a barbed-wire-enclosed compound used for storing brand-new cars. The cars are positioned in ranks, their strange colours – metallic oranges, vivid whites and azure blues – clashing with the elder and nettles that surround the compound's edges. As we leave Colchester the railway line passes a golf course, then large, irregularly shaped fields, thick woods, pylons. Occasionally branch rail tracks curve off into the distance, their banks lined with sycamore, ash, silver birch.

From Harwich to Bethnal Green the track, which was built

in the mid-1800s, is almost level. The Victorian engineers minimised its gradient by making cuttings into higher ground and raising the tracks over lower ground by building viaducts. The consequence of this is that some of the towns' stations are at ground level while others are raised above it. At Hatfield Peverel we can see directly into the surrounding houses, whereas at Chelmsford we are raised above them and so look down onto roofs, as well as parks with ponds. As we approach Liverpool Street the backs of houses begin to crowd together. The railway banks are covered in detritus – old sofas, plastic chairs, children's toys, all left to decompose among the spreading vegetation. Soon afterwards we pass the Olympic Park, with its fluid, red steel observation tower by Anish Kapoor, and the railway begins to gradually slope into the ground.

When we pass Bethnal Green we look down onto its park, watching children play and dogs run around below us. Then the track descends imperceptibly. Liverpool Street is 30ft below ground level and on the site of the old Bethlem Royal Hospital, or Bedlam, as it was known. As the tracks deepen, arched Victorian embankments made from brick keep back the weight of the surrounding city's earth. The tracks cut into the land. They pass under iron bridges and pavements and gardens and even at times through the foundations of buildings. Natural light falls away to a gloom. The bricks here remain uncleaned, still covered in soot from years ago, and the land is dotted with weeds. Small trees grow out of walls and beside the tracks. Tiny buildings with open doors and shattered glass are secreted underneath bridges. As we reach the deepest point the train slows and turns to its right, causing its wheels to squeal as they're forced against the rails' edges.

We leave the train, push our tickets through the stainless-steel barrier and walk onto the station's concourse to the first sculpture that commemorates the *Kindertransport*. It is by Flor Kent and is of two recently saved children gazing towards their futures, one standing, the other sitting next to a suit-case. We walk up two flights of stairs to the station's entrance on Liverpool Street itself and find the second sculpture that commemorates the *Kindertransport*. This is a companion piece to the statues at Bahnhof Friedrichstraße and the Hook of Holland, all by Frank Meisler. The one here is called 'Kindertransport – the Arrival'. A plaque next to it bears the statement from the Talmud: 'Whosoever rescues a single soul is credited as though they had saved the whole world.'

> You stood here when you got off the train?
> *We all assembled here. This is where it all started.*
> Incredible.
> *I became very worried because I was the very last person to be called.*

As it is Sunday morning there aren't many people around and so I lie down on my back on the station's concourse and stare at the station's roof. My father joins me, lying down beside me. Together we contemplate the wrought-iron spans, the flat plate glass, the walls made from London stock bricks, some faced with sandstone, the filigree cast-iron brackets. 'Must have been built around the same time as Bahnhof Berlin Friedrichstraße.' I take the photograph.

We get up off the floor, stand and take the Circle Line to Euston Square. We walk to Euston Station. My father will take the West Coast Main Line train to Crewe, change for Shrewsbury, then again for the Llanelli train, which stops at Llandrindod. Then he will take a taxi up the lane to his house.

Thanks for doing this trip, Dad.

I wanted to.

It was for Simon, wasn't it?

Yes.

We walk to the platform. We embrace. His grip is strong. I kiss him on the cheek. He does not kiss me back. We stand together, our awkward, stiff bodies fleetingly joined. He climbs on board the train with his crimson case. I see him through the window as he chooses his seat. I wave. He waves back. He looks happy as the train draws away from the platform.

Postscript

Jane rang me to tell me to come quickly. 'It won't be long now.' As I drove to see Hans my nerves gripped me. They spread from my stomach to my chest. They radiated along my arms and into my hands and then to the tips of my fingers. And so I became worried that my hands, which were gripping the steering wheel tightly, might, of their own accord, remove themselves from the wheel, leaving my car driverless and out of control – reminding me of Hans all those years ago.

And so it was with a sense of relief that I arrived a few hours later at the care home where Hans was being looked after. I walked through its small foyer, said hello to the nurse in charge, then walked down the short corridors to the room my father had been residing in for nearly a year. My mother and Jane were there, sitting, talking quietly to each other. Hans was lying in a bed next to them, on his side, turned to face them, shrunken, frail, breathing steadily, a strong, rasping breath.

Due to a particular idiosyncrasy of the care home's heating

system, the room my father was located in was always swelteringly hot. Whether due to a specific fault, or simply an inherent design error, the system pushed out tropical levels of heat. This, combined with the fact that the room's windows could only be opened an inch or two, meant that the room's air was oppressive.

I sat down in the wing-backed, rust-coloured chair situated next to my father's bed, leant forward and held his hand. His skin was delicate and, despite the heat of the room, his hand was cold. My mother, Jane and I talked quietly to each other. After an hour or so I drove my mother back to her house, a twenty-minute drive away. She had spent months visiting Hans every day and was now bone-tired. We talked as I drove, parked and walked into the house. Her feet were slow up the path, her hands and wrists fragile on the door handle, a wavering key finding the lock barrels to her front door, then a slow sinking into a chair. We drank tea, then I returned to the care home. Jane was still in the room, reading quietly, occasionally standing to kiss my father on his cheek – 'So brave.' She and I chatted together for an hour and then she left to go back to her house for a rest, leaving Hans and me alone.

Night fell. Although it was winter, the weather was temperate. Outside the window the branches of a large fir tree moved quietly. I went into the adjoining en-suite toilet and switched on the light above the sink. I returned to the main room, leaving the en-suite door slightly ajar. I switched off the main room's overhead lights. Light from the light above the sink in the en-suite toilet passed through the partially open door and lit Hans's room with a warm glow. His bed was placed against a wall and below a window. I leant across his body and pushed the window hard at its lowest edge. The safety catch that had been holding it sprung apart. The window opened several inches. Fresh air entered the room. Heated air left it. I pulled the wing-backed chair closer so that it touched Hans's bed.

I crossed my legs and meditated. I noticed the continual points of tension that I hold in my body, the fierce drill-like sensation inside the right side of my neck where my skull joins the first vertebrae, the burning sensation inside my right cheek, as though a hot needle is poking deep into the flesh, the dull ache around my kidneys, the sharp pains inside the top part of the socket of my left hip, the pain around the deformed vertebrae situated in my lower back, the noise of my own ears ringing. And I watched my thoughts rushing through my mind as best I could, trying not to judge them, not my fears, or the trivia of my thoughts, observing the moment as it was – not as I wanted it to be, not as I thought it should be, but as it was.

I could hear the wind moving quietly outside. I could hear the branches of the tree. I could hear the dysfunctional heating system disgorging gallons of hot water through itself – its fluid world circulating around us inside its pressed-steel radiators, pipes, valves and compression joints. I could hear the murmurings of people in other rooms, of doors opening and shutting, of trolleys being pushed along corridors. And if I opened my eyes I could see the photos of my father as a young man that my mother had pinned up beside his bed, running, parachuting, cycling, canoeing, sailing, piloting a plane, paragliding.

After sitting still for some time my body, all of a sudden, felt very different. A very dark and very cold shadow descended into it. An emptiness arrived. A void. A nothingness. I meditated with these sensations that were seemingly inside my body. They remained there for ten minutes or so. Then they passed away. My body became warm again. I had never felt such a cold thing inside me. I heard my father's breathing slow. I stood and placed my hand upon his chest. There was definitely a change in his breathing. I left the room, closed the door quietly and from the corridor outside his room rang Jane to tell her. I then went back into the room.

At 10 p.m. two nurses came to turn my father's body, as they always did, to prevent bedsores. They moved him from his side onto his back so that his head was now propped up by pillows. It was extremely difficult for him. He was semi-conscious but aware. His body was rigid. The movement seemed almost unbearable for him. After the nurses had left his breathing strengthened, his face became full of colour, his jaw determined. I could see life flowing through him. I stood next to him and placed my left hand on his head. It felt hot and full of energy. I placed my right hand on his chest. I said: 'I love you, Dad, I love you, Hans Eugen Lichtenstein – we've been on a journey together, you and I, and I love you very much. Thank you.' I kept my hands on his body and kissed his forehead. As I stood touching him his breath began to soften. I sang prayers. He began to take sips of air rather than rasps. His face relaxed. His skin smoothed. It became quite translucent. A gentle smile arrived on his mouth. His skin began to glow. Two tiny lights appeared, one on the top of his lip slightly to the right-hand side and one just below his lower lip in the middle. I scrutinised these lights for some time. I checked to see if it was the light coming from the en-suite bathroom but it wasn't. I could not work out where they were coming from, these lights that danced around his mouth for several minutes, bright needle pricks of light that moved. And then, as Hans's breathing quietened further I had a powerful sense of he and I being joined together. I understood we were both equal and that together he and I were repairing, during these moments, the link between us, the link that had been broken apart our whole lives.

And I understood too that my father was giving me a final gift. He was making death known to me. He was showing me what dying is. He was showing me that it is not frightening. He was showing me that it can be serene. He was showing me how it happens. That it is preceded by a cold shadow passing into the room. That the moment is tender. That fear is not a part of it. My guide – until his final moments. I bowed my head in thanks. And then during this surprising connection between us, while my hands rested upon both his head and his heart, his breathing slowed until it was no more and I stood in the room at peace. The fir tree moving outside the window. The sounds of the home. The room.

At this moment Jane arrived. She and I stood together next

to Hans as the final glimmers of his recognisable life ebbed away; his face now a gentle mask, his skin still warm but cooling, his jaw slightly open, his hands at rest upon the bedcovers.

Jane and I said little. We made a cup of tea. We drank it next to his now deceased body. We noticed his high cheekbones, the faint smile on his lips. After an hour or so we told the head night nurse. He rang 111 and went through the formal procedures that are gone through when a death is reported to the NHS over the phone. The nurse passed the phone to me. 'Was the death expected?' said the woman on the end of the line. 'Was it?' I thought to myself. 'Expected? Was the death expected?' I repeated to myself. 'Yes,' I answered, 'it was expected.' I had to give some details about Hans's date of birth, his place of birth and other formal information.

Jane and I drove back to my mother's house and woke her to tell her Hans had died. We sat next to her while she wept, holding both our hands. Her marriage had lasted for over sixty-three years. We stayed together for some time. She told us that at the end of their first date together in Kuala Lumpur they had talked for hours, long into the tropical evening and that, as he was driving her home, Hans had turned to her and said, 'It's a strange thing to say but I think we should get married,' and that she had known it too and had replied, 'Ask me again in a month.' During this conversation she told me something else – that after his return from our trip together to Berlin he had finally been able to sleep. The last years of his life had been more restful. We stayed up late. I slept at my parents' house.

The next day passed as though it was only an hour or two. Needing fresh air, I walked through the back door into the garden. I went out further, passing over the rusting steel of the cattle grid, with its rungs laid a foot above the land, past hedges with their dormant twigs of hawthorn, ash and beech. I walked for an hour or so along the lanes that descend into the valley until I came to the small footbridge that crosses the Ithon. I stepped onto the bridge and walked to its middle point where I stopped and, half leaning and half standing, held onto its wooden handrail. There I gazed up at the steep summit of Cefnllys hill that was now in front of me.

Below me the river flowed. I could hear its chatter. I felt a loosening in both my ankles. It was as though my feet were becoming disconnected from my body. Looking down, I could make out, through what was now becoming my undulating vision, no change in them. Despite the evidence of my eyes, it seemed that my ligaments and tendons were stretching, that they were in need of tightening and that in order to stop my feet detaching themselves and floating away into the air, and perhaps even into the upper sky that floated above me, and even beyond those heights, into the dark realms of space itself, I must do something to secure them. I leant more heavily against the bridge's handrail. My eyes focused upon the water below me. I saw several water skaters there, each with its broad feet resting on the river's surface, its hydrofuge body at ease upon the slowly flowing current. I began to bleed into the landscape. It was as though the cells and atoms of my body were disintegrating, that they were fusing into the air that surrounded me. Thoughts piled into my mind, the drawing of a water droplet when it was first seen under a microscope, the texture of a particular blanket I slept with as a child, the wings of a sparrow as they fluttered on a milk bottle, the taps of the kitchen in Pentrosfa, my father's smell, Walter's grave, the births of each of my three children, my wife's eyes. And I saw Simon walking towards me, smiling, upon the river, his arms outstretched, and I realised what has been said before: that we live not only with the memory of the dead and their haunting spectres, but within the dead's world, with their laying down of routes and roads, of hedges and bridges, of houses and dwellings, of farms and forests, of towns and cities, of monuments and great buildings, of their ideas and concepts, their philosophies and even their memories, so that we are all not just figuratively, but actually, living in the dead's minds.

And I became aware, again, of my own imminent passing. I came to understand that it was inevitable. I felt the fabric of the world's construction, so visibly apparent, yet made by so many of the long-dead.

And in this moment of estrangement from myself the world unfolded, a white spacious embrace in front of me, a fabulous vista, an extraordinary choreography, an almost infinite collection of small decisions made by those long gone, over billions of years, arriving at this particular moment, now and here. And all of them, the whole tapestry of them, teemed into me, and as they did so, I collapsed, gently, against the wooden handrail of the footbridge that passes over the Ithon.

Acknowledgements

Jonathan Conway, my literary agent, has nurtured this book from start to finish. His perceptive views, over many drafts, have helped shape its current form. My thanks go to him for his constant support. Both my editors at Scribner, Chris White and Rowan Cope, made incisive, vital observations at key points during the construction of the book and my thanks go to them for these, as well as their great good humour and continual encouragement. My thanks to Charlotte Chapman, for her wise and intuitive copy-editing, and to Kaiya Shang who has been such a constructive project editor.

My thanks too, to my theatre agents, Gemma Hirst and Katie Snaydon, at Gemma Hirst Agency. Their support, over many years, has been enormously helpful.

Simon Bacon, Nina Fischer, Kai Yin Low, Gabriel Pearson, Mike Roper and Steve Waters offered ideas about the material in *The Berlin Shadow*. My thanks go to all of them. I found Nina Fischer's book, *Memory Work: The Second Generation*, both eloquent and helpful. My thanks to Max Lichtenstein for encouraging Hans to make the journey to Berlin. I have worked with Shree Berke for many years. *The Berlin Shadow* is the result of her skill, kindness and care.

My thanks to the Leverhulme Trust whose research fellowship gave me the time to write *The Berlin Shadow* as well as providing funding for its research.

My thanks to my friends and family, especially Hans.

LEVERHULME
TRUST ⎯⎯⎯⎯

ENDNOTES

1. W. G. Sebald, 'Between History and Natural History', in Sebald, *Campo Santo*, trans. Anthea Bell (London, 2005), p. 73.
2. Ibid., p. 86.
3. Jean Améry, *At the Mind's Limits* (London, 1999), p. 25.
4. Ibid., p. 32.
5. Ibid., p. 33.
6. https://www.asymptotejournal.com/nonfiction/jean-amery-suicide-notes/